The F.I.X. Code

The Found Secret to Fixing My Life

Accepting the Past, Embracing the Future, & Living for Now

Cory Stickley

Copyright © 2019 Cory Stickley. All rights reserved. No portion of this book may be reproduced mechanically, electronically, or by any other means, including photocopying, without written permission of the publisher. It is illegal to copy this book, post it to a website, or distribute it by any other means without permission from the publisher.

Cory Stickley
70 Bruce St. South,
Thornbury, ON, Canada
N0H 2P0
705 607 1171

Limits of Liability and Disclaimer of Warranty

The author and publisher shall not be liable for your misuse of this material. This book is strictly for informational and educational purposes.

Warning – Disclaimer

The purpose of this book is to educate and entertain. The author and/or publisher do not guarantee that anyone following these techniques, suggestions, tips, ideas, or strategies will have the same results. The author and/or publisher shall have neither liability nor responsibility to anyone with respect to any loss or damage caused, or alleged to be caused, directly or indirectly by the information contained in this book.

"It is all about love."

To Beatrice, who summed up life so well.

Beautifully said, Mom!

If you enjoy this book, feel free to reach out to me at LivingAFixedLife@gmail.com.

Website: **thefixcode.com**

This book is about the F.I.X. Code, a metaphorical healing tool. It removes unconscious and unwanted emotions that run life without us being aware. It is a new type of healing modality that changed my life. You can find out more at **thefixcode.com.**

Stacey Nye's website: **staceynye.com**

Daniel Flear's website: **danielflear.com**

Contents

TESTIMONIALS 9

ACKNOWLEGEMENTS 11

PREFACE 13

INTRODUCTION 15
It Is Not About the Milk 15

PART ONE

CHAPTER 1 · SURPRISE! 19
Dealing with the Diagnosis 20
The Slow Road to Burnout 21
An Unexpected Assignment 24

CHAPTER 2 · THE RISE AND FALL OF MY CAREER 27
More Stress to Come 30
The Midterm Transfer 31

CHAPTER 3 · NOT THE JOB OF MY DREAMS 35

CHAPTER 4 · SEARCHING FOR ANSWERS 39
Frozen Operating System 41
How My Belief System Formed 43

CHAPTER 5 · A DIFFERENT FOCUS 47
Coping with Life 49

CHAPTER 6 · MY AH-HA MOMENT 53

CHAPTER 7 · MEET THE F.I.X. CODE FOUNDERS	57
CHAPTER 8 · I MEET STACEY NYE	61
Did You Have a Face Lift?	62
CHAPTER 9 · THE F.I.X. CODE IS NOT...	65
Stacey's Sad is Gone	66
CHAPTER 10 · WHY THE F.I.X. CODE IS DIFFERENT	69
Searching for Epiphany	70
CHAPTER 11 · COVER STORIES	75
You Are NOT Your Emotions	76
Reflect for a Moment	77
Keeping Anger at All Costs	78
CHAPTER 12 · EMOTIONS CAN BE CHANGED	81
FEARS AND ANXIETIES	83

PART TWO

CHAPTER 13 · AS WE GROW	87
No Filters from Birth to Seven	87
Adult Body—Childlike Emotions	88
Truly Growing Up	89
CHAPTER 14 · FEARS AND ANXIETY	91
Joanne's Piano	91
What Fear Looks and Feels Like	92
F.I.X. Code Session Two	93
Childhood Memories Become a Fear	94
My Fear Is Gone	95
CHAPTER 15 · FEAR OF FINANCIAL RUIN	97
Teasing this Apart	99
Fear of Financial Death	100
The Fear is Gone	102

CHAPTER 16 · ANGER 103
What Anger Looks and Feels Like 103
Benefits of Anger Gone 105

CHAPTER 17 · HURT 109
What Hurt Looks and Feels Like 109
Hurt Becomes Anger 113
Benefits of Hurt Gone 116

CHAPTER 18 · GUILT 119
What Guilt Looks and Feels Like 119
Benefits of Guilt Gone 121

CHAPTER 19 · SAD 125
What Sad Looks and Feels Like 125
Benefits of Sad Gone 127

CHAPTER 20 · BETRAYAL AND REJECTION 129
Raising Well-Adjusted Children 130
What Betrayal Looks and Feels Like 132
Micromanaging 135
Betrayal is a Double-Edged Sword 135
Rejection 138
Benefits of Betrayal Gone 138
A Musical Trigger for Betrayal 140

CHAPTER 21 · I'M A STUDENT AGAIN 143

REFERENCES 149

ABOUT CORY STICKLEY 150

Testimonials for Stacey Nye and The F.I.X. Code

"Have you seen the ads for the F.I.X. Code and thought, *Here we go again—another ad targeting my vulnerabilities!* If so, then know you are not alone. If it wasn't for the fact that I have known Stacey for years and know that her intentions have always come from a place of caring and honor I would have missed out on a healing modality that has finally shut down the emotional codes that I have used for almost 60 years.

"Believe me when I say that I was gob smacked by how quickly these codes where released from my mind. I am both a Reiki Master and a Practitioner of Emotional Release work through the Chakras and I know from personal experience how long and draining it is to try to touch base with a client and bring forward the emotional baggage that is holding them back. So to find a technique that is beautiful in both its seemingly simple visuals and language that works NOW and leaves you, the client, at peace and also enervated at the same time is Amazing.

"I am so thankful to both Daniel and Stacey for taking the jump and the years of work to bring this F.I.X. Code to everyone. I encourage you all to give it a try!"

—Debra Rae

"I just realized something this morning. Using the F.I.X. Code has made me more courageous. Normally, when I get bad feelings, I just want them to go away. I ignore them or sugar coat them with affirmations I don't really believe in. But having the F.I.X. Code, I look at those feelings and deal with them because I know I can get rid of them. As well as helping me feel a million times better, the F.I.X. Code gives me courage to work through the muck that life dishes out."

—S. J.

"I honestly feel different after our F.I.X. Code session. I have always felt a gnawing ache—deep inside—ever since I can remember. It's always with me—deep underneath—even if I'm laughing my head off (if that makes sense), but...that seems to be gone! I'm almost afraid to write this in case it suddenly reappears. I feel so much lighter. Thank you!"

—M.M.

"After my first session, my life was followed by 6–8 months of pure bliss. I have never felt that good. Every single area in my life improved dramatically. The part I like the best is being to heal from emotional damage. I would recommend the F.I.X. Code to everybody to try at least once in their lives. We endure too much needless suffering. The most important thing in working with the F.I.X code is to know that you can feel the way you have always wanted."

—Brian

Acknowledgements

I'D LIKE TO ACKNOWLEDGE the influence of all who have crossed my path in this lifetime. That very act of meeting you, has affected me in some way that I may not be aware of or able to speak about. This includes but is not limited to my husband Don, family, friends, colleagues, students, my own teachers. As I reflect, I am aware that each encounter has been an opportunity to grow.

Specifically related to this book, I'd like to thank my editor, Donna Kozik, for guidance, patience, and encouragement throughout the process. Donna and her design team have made this book a reality.

My heartfelt thanks go to Daniel Flear and Stacey Nye who have generously shared their knowledge and information with me. Without their work to bring the F.I.X. Code to light, this book would never have been written. This is an extraordinary journey.

Thank you.

Preface

POISED AT THE BEDROOM DOORWAY, heart pounding, the five-year-old took a giant leap toward the far side of the room, toes touching the floor only twice. She landed in a heap on her bed, all in one piece.

This was her nightly routine. Under her bed lived an imaginary lion that represented all her childhood fears: being afraid of the dark or left alone, separated from her parents, or having the house burn down.

Hanging over the edge, she peeked under the bed, but it appeared the sleeping lion had not heard her. While she had never seen the lion, she was convinced he was there. She slept soundly, safe until the next bedtime.

It seemed that lion had always lived there. It was necessary to be quiet, fast, and under the covers before he woke up. It was kind of a game she played—her imagination knew no bounds. She believed in fairies and the magic of Peter Pan, but the invisible lion was scary.

Two years later, the imaginary lion moved to a new town with them and again slept under the bed.

Introduction

IT IS NOT ABOUT THE MILK

8 a.m. There was no milk in the house after her breakfast, so Jan asked Bill to pick some up on the way home after work. He agreed.

Jan wasn't sure he would. The last few times she'd asked for him to help out, he had forgotten. She didn't trust him to remember. Betrayal is one of Jan's emotional codes that unconsciously runs her life. As a five-year old, the fighting and name calling of her parents' marriage had made a life-long impression on her. She had witnessed their silences and anger.

Today, working from home, she will be unable to take the time to go out. She knows there is a chance Bill will forget to bring home the milk. Midmorning, Jan texts a reminder.

"Don't forget the milk."

"I've got this."

2 p.m. Jan texts again, "It's the lactose-free milk with the blue label." She doesn't get a response, so she continues to fret while she makes her phone calls.

3:30 p.m. Jan dashes to the corner store and picks up the milk.

5:30 p.m. Bill walks in carrying the milk. An argument begins, "What is going on? I said I'd pick up the milk, and I did. Do you think I'm an idiot? I don't need all those reminders. It's milk!"

Bill is now angry and hurt that Jan thinks he's so stupid he can't remember milk. It is an unpleasant evening. But this is only beginning. Next week, she asks Bill once again, to pick up milk. Taking a chance, trusting he would do as promised, she doesn't text or pick up milk.

Bill walks in without the milk. He'd had a busy day and forgot. Jan is fully armed for battle, and the argument was brutal — apparently all over milk.

"What is wrong with you? All we needed was one quart of milk. What is so difficult about that!" The battle stance, loud voice, and name calling convince Bill to retreat.

You know this isn't over yet, don't you?

Weeks later, Jan asks Bill to pick up a few items at the store on the way home. He is still annoyed about the names she called him. It hasn't been pleasant at home. Jan believes she has to remind him because he has forgotten before. Today she sends him three reminders.

But, today is different. Bill has internalized that Jan doesn't trust him, he is hurt and angry and chooses to ignore the texts. On the way home, he realizes he has to go out of his way to run the errand. Jan likely picked up the items because she believes he is an idiot. He makes a conscious decision to not go to the store. In his head, he is actually having a conversation that goes like, "If you are so smart, then go to the store yourself."

The relationship is deteriorating. Jan has micromanaged her partner into feeling useless, stupid, unreliable. Neither understands what is happening. Each blames the other for making life unpleasant. It has been impossible to hide this from the children who are now acting out and refusing to do as they are asked.

THE F.I.X. CODE

Everyone is on edge, not knowing if their words or actions will start an argument. Nothing they do seems to be right.

We will meet this family later to see where this story goes.

Part One

· CHAPTER 1 ·

Surprise!

DR. DONAHUE ENTERED THE ROOM with my medical file open in her hand. She made her way behind her desk, still reading. Whatever I thought she was going to tell me, I was unprepared for her actual words.

"You must take six weeks off work to rest. You are not to have any contact with your school—no phone calls, emails, work dropped off. You have burned out and cannot continue at this pace. Your test results are barely okay but not for much longer. Your cortisol levels are off the charts, which means possible adrenal fatigue. If you don't get this under control, you are headed for a major disease."

Stunned, I sat trying to absorb this. There had been talk of adrenal fatigue in the past, but I had not understood these consequences.

She continued, "Here's a prescription for adrenal support

supplements. Take as directed. I am referring you to a psychiatrist for evaluation and counseling. Come back in six weeks. We'll redo the tests and see how you are progressing."

Dealing with the Diagnosis

Ironically, the diagnosis of burnout led to more problems — something else I had to do. I was to leave my position as school principal immediately. There would be upheaval and stress as staff were reorganized to cover my duties. I was conflicted about taking any time off but knew there was little choice. I was not capable of continuing.

To be involved with the daily operations would increase my stress level, possibly resulting in a major disease such as cancer or heart attack. Even that news didn't mean much in the moment. I planned to return in six weeks. I was optimistic.

My doctor called it burnout. In shock, I had not even asked what that meant. I understood that I needed some rest. While on sick leave, I slept on the sofa all day, went to bed at night and slept some more. I had never been so exhausted in my life. My face was tired. My teeth ached. My bones were weary. My mind was fuzzy. It was an enormous effort to get dressed. I did no housework or cooking. I had no energy.

Since I wasn't capable of much, I had plenty of time to think about what I should have been doing at work. Because of my abrupt departure, important projects had been left unfinished, piled on my desk, and were now the VP's responsibility.

School organization is a massive project that starts in April. New staff would be interviewed and hired, class timetables planned, next year's classes arranged. It was a hectic schedule that included many after-hours meetings. In addition, the end of a school year is already busy with student promotions, report cards, and special events like graduation.

I was confident that I'd be back at school to work on all the organizing once the doctor approved my return to work in May.

I was wrong.

In May, the doctor now advised me to remain on leave until the end of September. When I questioned why she hadn't told me this from the beginning, she replied, "I knew you'd never agree."

She was right.

Even after these six weeks off work, I was still completely empty inside—a hologram of myself—an outline with no feelings, passion, interests, or personality. As much as I wanted to be at work—supporting, caring, helping, doing my job—it was not possible.

This leave of absence stretched into fifteen months, finally ending in my resignation. I had not seen that coming.

Even after these six weeks off work, I was still completely empty inside—a hologram of myself—an outline with no feelings, passion, interests, or personality

---

THE SLOW ROAD TO BURNOUT

My stress had begun to build many years earlier. It is evident now that my only coping strategy was to keep moving forward. I ignored any fears or anxieties. I had been told, "This too shall pass." Yes, the event ended, but the stress did not.

I wanted to quit the Faculty of Education. I had a suspicion this was not my calling. My parents said, "We never thought of you as a quitter." At that time, women's careers were limited to teaching, nursing, or secretarial work. It was a significant moment—I recall the feeling of "not having a choice" when I reluctantly decided to continue my training. Not wanting to disappoint them, I graduated and applied for a teaching position.

It was a significant moment—I recall the feeling of "not having a choice" when I reluctantly decided to continue my training.

A new graduate wishing to become a teacher must survive the first five years of the job to become certified. There are major challenges as they adjust to a new home and routines, a heavy workload, expectations of students, parents, and administration. It seemed like a rite of passage for them to be given the worst assignments, poorly-equipped classrooms, and limited support. Sink or swim. Do or die. The pressure is so great that many quit before the five years are up.

I worked long hours all week, then socialized with staff, relaxed, did creative work or yoga, windsurfed, and went to auctions. On winter weekends, I skied. I began to experience tension headaches and was forced to take a time off occasionally. I loved my class of gifted students, but the work environment started to affect my health.

Because I did not know what anxiety was, I accepted my panic attacks as a normal part of meeting new challenges and ignored the signals my body was giving me.

Ironically, after four years, I quit. I became a statistic.

I moved to a new city, married, and opened a small decorating business—all major stressors. A year later, I made a spur-of-the-moment choice between growing my business or going back to teaching and doing what I had trained for. Again, I ignored those past warning signs about stress.

This work culture was a new challenge because of the inner-city designation, but declining enrolment forced the closure of numerous schools. Teachers hired last were fired first. The official term was "redundant"—it meant fired.

For the next eight years, my contract was terminated each May. I was rehired in September, bouncing from one school to another, one position to another, one part of the city to another—wherever administration placed me. It was the same for most surplus staff, but I was fortunate to have qualifications that were in demand. Other "numbered" teachers were moved more often than I was or divided their time between three schools each day.

One year, I taught English as a Second Language for a month; the remainder of the year, I worked with learning disabled children. Another year, I taught a pilot program for ten children whose learning disabilities were compounded by a diagnosis like autism, ADHD, or behavioral issues. I was not prepared for the students' anger or the verbal and physical abuse my teaching partner and I were exposed to. In this one year, without changing my eating habits, I gained forty pounds. The stress piled on along with the weight.

Another year, I traveled throughout the school system to test and diagnose children with severe learning disabilities. It was an intense process involving writing lengthy reports. There was little contact with people and while this honed my diagnostic skills, it was not satisfying work. If I wanted to teach, I had no option but to hang in there each year despite the increasing level of stress.

An Unexpected Assignment

It's hard to believe, but little did I realize that all that changing of schools and assignments was not healthy. People were not as aware of the effects of stress as they are now, and they didn't discuss it. After working in ten different schools over four years, I was placed in a school where I would remain for several years, only because parents petitioned to keep me there. I would be part of a school community once again.

I had trained to teach English in high school, so imagine my surprise at being assigned to a Grade One class. The Human Resources superintendent assured me that I would love the job. How could he predict that? What was he thinking? Grade One was the last place I wanted to be.

"Help, Michelle! I have no idea what to do with twenty-five six-year-old kids for an hour, let alone a whole day. You are an expert. Please, can you help?"

My friend came to the rescue, coaching me on setting up an activity-based program. By February, I loved the children and the program. Together we welcomed teachers from other school districts who wanted to observe what first-graders were capable of. With my guidance, the children ran the classroom.

Being with six-year-olds as they learn to read and write was exhilarating. Their enthusiasm each morning inspired me. Challenging their minds and satisfying their curiosity was one of the most rewarding jobs ever. How they processed information was fascinating. We played, imagined, sang, laughed, and loved learning. We incubated chicken eggs and watched them hatch. We hosted a family craft night, young authors' conferences, produced a weekly newspaper, and planned Games Day for the school. The classroom was alive with active learning.

It was during my time here that I met Jan. In the Introduction, you met her as an adult, but I met her as a six-year-old whose parents were divorcing. My heart went out to her. She wore her sadness like a cloak. Jan could be close to tears one moment and in the next, confused and challenging, escalating her attention-getting behavior by being funny or tugging at my sleeve. On Mondays, after weekends with Dad or when Mom's new boyfriend was around, her mood was unpredictable. She believed no one wanted her, so that is why they shared her.

Jan was one of several students in the class whose parents separated. I admired these children who faced their situations with courage, knowing that the classroom was a safe, predictable place to be. That was my job. Keep them safe, be predictable with my affection, discipline, and interactions—all while teaching them.

At the urging of a colleague whose child had flourished while in my room, I took my principal certification courses with the intention of bringing the same commitment to a whole school, not just one classroom. Jan and her classmates continued on to the next grade, and I left that school.

For a year, I worked as a union leader negotiating pay equity settlements and contracts. When I applied for a vice principal's position, I was accepted for the interview process and promoted partly because of my broad range of teaching experience. It's ironic how all that stressful changing of schools and variety of assignments would eventually be beneficial.

· CHAPTER 2 ·

The Rise and Fall of My Career

AFTER TWO YEARS AS A VICE PRINCIPAL in a tough part of the city, I was thrilled to be promoted to principal in a K-5 school only blocks from my home. As one of the few female administrators in a male dominated role, it went without saying that I would have to prove myself capable of the job.

I was energetic and enthusiastic. This was the kind of job I envisioned. I could truly make a difference in many lives. I'd bound out of bed, excited to begin my day, and arrive very early to be available to staff. So many problems could be solved informally in the hallways or staffroom when teachers gathered to have coffee, seek advice, and relax.

Staff morale was high, and that affects everything. When visitors entered the school, they commented on the warm, vibrant, welcoming atmosphere—exactly what we wanted.

It was such a joy to interact with students. I was often greeted with hugs from the younger students during classroom visits as they gathered to show me their latest work. My office walls were decorated with student gifts of paintings and handwritten cards. How could a job be this much fun?

> *How could a job be this much fun?*

As a team, we introduced innovative school-wide programming, which earned us a reputation for excellence. Because of my strong background in curriculum, I encouraged staff to implement current research on learning. There was a waiting list for families living outside our boundaries wanting to enroll their children.

For several years, I thrived on the unpredictable daily workflow and the ongoing interaction with staff and students and community. I loved that part of my work, but there were many other components of this job. I worried about the students who had problems. During parent interviews, much private information is shared. The details of those conversations were on my mind at night as I searched for solutions for the families.

One of the most stressful responsibilities involved overseeing staff and writing annual performance reports. What a joy to confirm that staff are well placed; what a challenge if there are competence issues. This cannot be avoided, either morally or legally. Students are entitled to the best education possible. I took this duty very seriously.

Counseling teachers to leave the profession was difficult. It was usually adversarial and could end up in court. So much of my work was confidential that I will not write about it even now. During such times, my stress level increased. I routinely worked twelve-hour days, which affected my health. I was able to cope as well as I did because of a strong personal support system.

But about the same time, my personal life became a major source of stress. My father—a former Air Force navigator and aeronautical engineer—was showing unusual cognitive and personality changes. He was struggling for words, using phrases like "subterranean room" for basement.

When he and Mom arrived two hours late for lunch one weekend, his first angry words were, "None of the cars would move over to let me exit. I had my signals on. Ignorant city drivers!" When he was able to exit the highway, the man with an unfailing sense of direction had gotten lost.

Weeks later, the doctor at the geriatric clinic diagnosed him with Alzheimer's and immediately took his driver's license. He was not allowed to drive home that day. After driving safely for sixty-five years, he expressed his shock and anger at the injustice of this. My mother was visibly shaken as this confirmed some of her suspicions about his recent behavior. Their lives changed significantly in that moment.

Mom had to be vigilant. One night around 2 a.m. when she heard the back door close, she discovered that Dad had found the hidden set of car keys. He was preparing to drive thirty miles to the airport, believing he was to meet my sister at "Arrivals." Keeping an eye on him 24/7 became a full-time job. It is an understatement to say he didn't take kindly to supervision.

As their Power of Attorney for Personal Care, I became involved in their health care decisions and appointments.

Thankfully, my sister was able to return to the country to share this responsibility.

Within months, Dad moved into a nursing home. My mother's debilitating chronic pain was diagnosed as cancer. She was in hospice for six weeks and died in December. Although my father lived for three more years, I was grieving the loss of both parents that Christmas.

More Stress to Come

One month later in January, Human Resources informed me that I was being transferred midyear to a new school. The news was to be kept secret for a month while I prepared to exit this school, yet keeping up appearances that all was normal—meanwhile mourning my family and packing.

I was also grieving the loss of my school. I had grown to love the students and respect their parents. I lived in this community. At Halloween, I admired their costumes when they knocked on my door. I saw their parents in the grocery store, and we ate next to each other at the restaurant. It was here that Jan visited to tell me she had left home and quit school.

Principals were routinely moved to schools where their skills were needed. That was no consolation; I felt like a pawn in a chess game. This feeling added to the stress from my personal life as I was now preparing to sell my parents' home.

Eventually I was permitted to share the news of my transfer with staff, who were shocked. A week later, I said a tearful goodbye to my work family of dear colleagues, students, parents, and a community I had served for seven years. It was another loss.

When I arrived at my new school, I was truly sad, yet I was not one to shirk my duty. There was a job to be done. Would I find my passion again?

A week later, I said a tearful goodbye to my work family of dear colleagues, students, parents, and a community I had served for seven years. It was another loss.

THE MIDTERM TRANSFER

I was grieving during this whole period. My life must have been a mess although I didn't see it as such. I believed I adjusted to each incremental increase in stress. If I had seen a list of major stressors and the resulting physical effects on our health, I might have been more concerned. I didn't have time to worry about such things.

I went to work each day. I put one foot in front of the other. At day's end, I was drained and exhausted. Any moments of enthusiasm and energy could not be sustained. Never did I consider there might be something wrong nor did it cross my mind to see a doctor until much later. There was no time for relaxing. I had engaged a real estate agent to sell my parent's home. Each weekend I sorted a lifetime of family memories and possessions—keeping some, discarding others.

Some staff at the new school had welcomed my arrival; others were not so sure. My reputation preceded me—president of the women teachers' union, contract and pay equity negotiator, workshop leader, conference speaker, advocate of women's rights, innovative teacher, champion for children. In addition, I was a female principal in a male dominated profession. It was inevitable that there would be changes in the way the school was run. Once again, I prepared to demonstrate that I was more than capable.

The student body at this inner-city K-8 school represented countries from around the world. They spoke fifty-two different dialects. There was a class of medically-challenged students awaiting heart transplants or suffering from severe seizure disorder or life-threatening chronic diseases. The socio-economic levels ranged from poverty to upper middle class. As a community school, there was additional staff from the Parks and Recreation Department to collaborate with.

Children who were refugees from war-torn countries bringing with them hatred, resentment, and fears now sat in class beside perceived enemies. Tensions often erupted over foreign language slogans on tee shirts. Reaching a solution with the students was a time-consuming process.

A favorite part of my job, visiting classrooms to interact with students was no longer possible with my new schedule. I was focused on many behavioral issues. Lengthy interviews with parents who could be verbally abusive while defending their child's behavior took up much of my time.

The job had evolved into one I had not signed on for—office management, budgeting, and running interference. Not the best use of my skills; it was not my passion. But it had to be done, and so I soldiered on with the help of a secretary and part-time vice principal. There were not enough hours in the day to get everything done. I was run ragged.

Below this paragraph is a list of some of the common stressors we all face at some time or other. Perhaps you are familiar with some of them. They are not in any particular order—they are all a big deal.

> ## Common Stressors
>
> - Death of a family member
> - Marriage, divorce, separation
> - Having a child
> - Problems with your child at school
> - Bankruptcy, worries about money
> - Moving
> - Hospitalization, chronic illness, or injury
> - Emotional problems (depression, anxiety, anger, grief, guilt, low self-esteem)
> - Caring for an elderly relative
> - Problems sleeping
> - Abuse
> - Legal problems
> - Feeling powerless in your job
> - Being fired
> - Conflict at work
> - Unemployment
> - Commuting
> - Retirement
> - Bankruptcy, worries about money
> - Traumatic events: natural disaster, war, theft, attack
>
> **SOURCES:** WEBMD.COM, WWDPI.ORG, PAINDOCTOR.COM

CHAPTER 3

Not the Job of My Dreams

Little by little, it became more difficult to find joy in my work. Occasionally I could schedule a visit to a classroom to participate in the excitement of learning. Several teachers would frequently send students to share their projects with me. Those were the bright moments. I did not bound out of bed each morning—instead I dragged myself to work. Little things became an annoyance, and I handled imposed change poorly.

When Administration requested intensive, time-consuming new procedures for tracking special needs students, I was appalled. That was twenty percent of my students. How would I find time to do as requested? At a meeting of a hundred colleagues, I was the only one to ask, "Which of my current duties can I eliminate?"

None.

I was overwhelmed, angry inside, fighting for my life. But not one friend or colleague expressed concern to me until long after I had gone down in flames.

My lunch was often interrupted to solve problems. Hours later, with a pounding headache, I'd notice the half-eaten lunch where I'd forgotten it on the staff room table. I was not paying attention to my health, not eating well and I was gaining weight!

My sense of humor disappeared. I no longer looked forward to each day with anticipation. After a twelve-plus hour day, I dragged myself home. My husband would cook dinner when I walked through the door at 9 p.m. I fell into bed, slept fitfully, problem-solving all night long, and woke up tired.

I had become more emotional than usual. So much sad news came my way, much of it not my responsibility, but people have always confided in me. In one fairly typical workday, I learned that one of my students was awaiting a heart transplant, and I spent two hours in conversation with a staff member whose step-mother was terminally ill with the same disease her mother had died from.

I felt like I carried the weight of the world on my shoulders. I would become teary-eyed when telling parents their child needed special help. My blood pressure soared, and my heart pounded when addressing the assembled student body. I ignored my anxiety in order to do my job, but I wasn't thinking clearly. I made mistakes, felt short tempered, and forgot important details.

Writing notes to myself helped a bit with the memory problem if I could keep track of the lists. My bulletin board became littered with to-do notes, one on top of the other. My Day-Timer, a critical organizational tool, became a reminder of incomplete projects. I moved non-essential tasks forward from one week to the next to the next before finally ignoring them. Trying to stay organized was increasingly difficult.

This school had a caring staff that worked hard to problem

solve with their students before referring them to me. But because of my stress level, the balance scales seemed tipped so that eighty percent of my time was spent with the least satisfying twenty percent of the work.

One year after being transferred to this school, I went to see my doctor for the first time about my low energy. You know how that played out. Yes, she advised me to take a leave of absence. It began with six weeks off—fifteen months later, I resigned.

I discovered how empty I was, unable to find any emotion in myself, not even anger—I felt flat and lifeless. Even after several months on sick leave, the thought of being back at work caused intense anxiety and fear. I did not want to see anyone I knew, let alone stand in front of the whole student body, staff, and curious parents. I felt exposed and vulnerable.

I was embarrassed at how I was not strong enough to do my job, at leaving others to pick up the pieces. I felt guilty for being weak. I was angry at myself for not being able to finish what I started. Remember how my own parents had instilled in me that I was not a quitter? That did not work out very well, did it?

When I finally resigned, the unofficial diagnosis was PTSD, a label not commonly used outside the military at that time. It never occurred to me that my life had been anything like war. Now, when I read about the symptoms of PTSD, I see the signs.

My fears of not surviving had come true. When I consider that I had limited coping skills, this is no surprise. What strategies I had were from observing how others close to me hid problems, kept a stiff upper lip, didn't talk about important issues or ask for help.

> *I was angry at myself for not being able to finish what I started.*

I never returned to the education system. I used to regret not having had a chance to personally thank the staff for ensuring the school continued to run smoothly. My leaving would have been disruptive in many ways.

My exit was one of those scenarios that people discuss in hushed tones—wondering what the real story was. They asked, "What deadly disease did she have?"

"Did she do something wrong?"

"Did she have a break down? Is she mentally ill?"

"Is she dying?"

"Why didn't she say goodbye?"

"Was she fired?"

"When is she coming back?"

Those were the questions parents asked if we met on the street. I never knew what the school community had been told about my leaving. For months I hid myself from the world, safe inside my home, not wanting to face any one. Never would I have predicted such an untimely, awkward, embarrassing end to a career I had loved.

How in the world had I sunk so low?

· CHAPTER 4 ·

Searching for Answers

I was so overwhelmed that I didn't realize I was in danger. As long as I was able to put one foot in front of the other, I thought I was doing okay. I didn't know any better. I didn't take the time to consider if there was another way to live my life. It felt like there were no options.

I had accepted that this was my life. Each decision appeared to be a solution that would get me out of the quagmire, but it never did. There was always another problem to be solved, hurdle to jump, fearful situation to face at work and at home. The pressure was relentless.

This situation was beyond my skill as a problem solver. None of the solutions I had tried over the years worked. It was almost impossible to make wise decisions when I felt this way.

Looking back at all that happened, it seems to me that the problems originated with childhood events—habits, beliefs and fears. These determined my values, my choice of career, my interpretation of a good life, and my purpose in the world. When children are young, it takes little to make an impression on them, which may set them up for a fear or mistaken beliefs about themselves.

When children are young, it takes little to make an impression on them, which may set them up for a fear or mistaken beliefs about themselves.

For example, when a sibling is thought to be favored by a parent, feelings of being not worthy of love or not good enough are only two of many emotions that can result. A game of hide and seek when father helps one player hide may be interpreted as favoritism or betrayal. This makes a lasting impression. A child doesn't understand adult rationale just because the parent has the power to act. Before the age of seven, children have no filters, and they interpret events at face value. Adults have reasons for their decisions, but a young child won't understand without explanation. Even that may be insufficient.

No one else was raised as I was. I don't expect that my experiences will be understood by everyone. But in some way, you may know the feelings and have comparable situations.

I was totally unprepared for this chapter in my life—the stress and burning out followed by my resignation. This exposed childhood fears and anxieties that I couldn't identify at the time but have since learned were issues like fear of failure, abandonment, and fear of dying, as well as guilt, overcompensating behaviors, and the feeling of betrayal.

I was tired of fighting, feeling imposed upon, angry, hurt and feeling used by my superiors. A mashup of my childhood fears had followed me to adulthood. This was my imaginary lion springing to life, but I didn't have the insight to be afraid.

Frozen Operating System

I can usually find several solutions to a problem, but this burnout was like a frozen operating system on a computer. What had worked for me in the past was so outdated, like having Windows 3 when I needed Windows 10. I crashed. I had ignored my inner voice for too long, assuming I would get through this rocky patch of life.

Treating my problems ostrich style didn't work and neither did self-help books. That was disappointing. Counseling and talk therapy sessions similar to those I had recommended to colleagues identified issues but did not solve them.

The psychiatrist had been convinced I had some life issues to work on. I had to agree. But again, there were no solutions. Exhausted, numb, submissive, beaten down—after resigning from my job, it was another two years before I felt human again.

Even years later, stressful situations can cause anxiety, high blood pressure, and poor memory. These are warning signs that I need to change my current coping strategy.

I have always found inspiration in books, so I read those by James Hollis, Deepak Chopra, Carl Jung, Helen Luke, Robert Johnson, Wayne Dyer, Marianne Williamson, and Eckhart Tolle to name a few. My library expanded rapidly as one self-help book led to another in my search for wholeness. I embraced their messages, but what was missing was how to accomplish what they advocated.

When that didn't help, I searched in other directions.

As best as I could, I sang hymns, participated in ceremonies, held hands of strangers, was hypnotized, bonded through shared experiences, burned incense and candles, had my thoughts and actions scrutinized, wore special jewelry, chanted, drummed, did yoga and tai chi, studied violin, sang in choirs, tithed, meditated, served selflessly, journaled, and traveled to sacred sites where others had searched.

I had been counseled, sought advice, examined my childhood, interpreted my dreams, did vision boards and affirmations, did energy work, had tarot readings, prayed, sat cross legged, fasted, feasted, donated, volunteered, sacrificed for others…and would do it all again. I was committed to each activity, but there was no lasting answer to my searching.

In desperation, I sought a non-traditional healer for support, training, and to be in service, hoping this was the solution. Her retreats revealed a side of life that I had never had time to explore before. I gained insight into the metaphysical world. I examined my path from a Jungian perspective. As a group of modern-day pilgrims guided by our teacher on our own quest, we walked the labyrinth at Chartres Cathedral in France. We explored the ancient Greek temples in Delphi and Crete, meditated in the ruins of mystery schools in Delos and the tholos at Epidaurus—always carrying our own soul-searching questions.

Still questing, I journeyed to Zimbabwe with a group of healers and lived with a Shona healer and his family for twenty days participating in unfamiliar rituals, traveling to Victoria Falls and Great Zimbabwe, their ancient holy city. We met the wise woman, a mystical healer who knew intuitively that we would arrive a day later than planned. There was so much of life I didn't understand.

Each healing modality I heard of seemed worth pursuing and moved me forward but I did not find the all encompassing path to wholeness. This was all worthwhile but not sufficient. Nothing seemed to last or bring about the much-needed changes I sought, and I blamed myself for the lack of success.

How My Belief System Formed

So much of what we think, feel, and believe as adults has come to us through the filtered ideas of people who were in our lives as we grew up. I certainly accepted my parents as my authority in life, never questioning their wisdom or advice. As a young child, I took each day in its turn.

I have become aware of patterns of interaction and responses that were put in place while I was a toddler. That is why I say, "It really is not my fault I feel angry." But now that I'm aware of this, I need to deal with it.

This may sound convenient and cliché, but it is important. With current belief that up to eighty percent of our makeup is passed down through DNA and so little of it through nurturing, much of our belief system, personality traits, and emotions are with us when we arrive in the world. We have the personality traits of our ancestors, not just our parents. Let me explain how it seems to work.

Each generation passes on to the next its wisdom, cultural beliefs, and practices. Much of this is done through nurturing but, depending on what you read, not all of it can be attributed to that. Studies on twins and triplets separated at birth show similarities in hobbies, personalities, and interests that cannot be due to how they were raised. I have observed fraternal twins raised by their natural parents and am fascinated by the differences and similarities in personality and interests.

My own DNA is a result of my parents' genetic makeup, which was passed down from their parents. While I may not have the exact same personality tendencies as my grandparents, there can be similarities just as there are physical characteristics.

My grandmother's five children moved to various parts of North America and seldom saw each other as adults. When their children, the cousins, connected as adults, it was fascinating to hear of two who had taken violin lessons as adults because they couldn't ignore the longing to play that instrument. Others shared similar mannerisms, facial expressions, strong math skills, and interests in science, technology, and architecture. Several had a talent for writing that seemed to stretch back several generations. The physical traits they shared were more obvious: the shape of their hands, facial features, and tone of voice. It was the not-so-obvious family traits that were intriguing.

My father was the "brick wall" disciplinarian and was to be obeyed, which meant the children had no voice. We loved him but also lived in fear of crossing the line. The fear was worse than the actual outcome. There was no discussion. What he said was the law in the house. That was how he had been raised.

My mother often used the phrase, "Wait until your father is home." This meant she was avoiding the unpleasant task of discipline or didn't know how to deal with it which made her appear weaker. I believed men had the power.

Society began to challenge these standards during the 1970s

and 80s, but by then my belief system was well entrenched. The practices of raising children changes with each generation. While the issues may change, the emotional root causes seem to be similar.

My parents were born into families where the older children looked after younger ones. Following this tradition, I was given much responsibility for my younger sister. I was to make sure she was safe, help her, walk her to school. Being responsible at an early age for another human being whom my parents loved was more responsibility than a child needs. We developed a love hate relationship, giving consolation and support at times while struggling with sibling rivalry, fighting for parental attention, and wrestling with our fears—some of which lived under the bed disguised as an imaginary lion.

I internalized all of this. Over time, it grew into an overwhelming burden of responsibility. It formed a core value and belief that has taken years to reduce to a manageable size. As an adult, I felt responsible for most people and events in my life. This became unmanageable, out of proportion, and damaging to my health. During my career, each year I was responsible for a class full of students, and as principal, for staff and many more students. The responsibility never seemed to end.

Being responsible for a younger sibling robbed me of some childhood freedom. When my mom went to work outside the home, my responsibility for my sister was extended to after school and summer week days. I had a serious job.

> *As an adult, I felt responsible for most people and events in my life.*

I unconsciously made her the priority in my life. I thought it was what sisters did but discovered as an adult that this was not a healthy relationship.

Often our early lessons in life came by default from overhearing conversations about cousins or neighbors' children: "I don't know what got into that one; he should know better." This implied that our behavior should not mimic his.

All of this was open to the misinterpretation of a child who couldn't really know or understand what the offender had done wrong. We didn't see the whole picture, so these lessons made us fearful of making mistakes and being rejected.

Young children have no filters. Life events need to be discussed and explained so children can learn valuable lessons. I had learned long ago not to ask questions so I internalized a lot of misinformation. That is part of the reason I say, "It is not my fault."

From these scenarios came the negative emotions. You will recognize many of them: the feeling of not being heard, angry at not having a voice, fear of abandonment or rejection, always being told what to do, not listened to, being unsure and very responsible, second guessing my own behavior, anger at unfairness and empathy for the victim, feeling taken advantage of, being used, lacking courage to be myself, dumbing down intelligence, not outshining the boys, and the list goes on. Maybe you have had similar feelings.

None of what I did over the years solved my problems. My life looked good from outside. Still searching for a rich inner life, I began to photograph at the sacred sites I visited, finding some inspiration and a sense of peace.

· CHAPTER 5 ·

A Different Focus

By this time it appeared to me that I needed to work through the difficult parts, and life would be better—and it was. I was naïve. I had no idea how huge this task would be once I started. I also didn't realize that other people had similar fears and challenges. People didn't discuss their problems. I was on my own.

Photography had always been a hobby. I had my first camera when I was about seven or eight. But now I pursued this with an intense passion. I upgraded from my 35mm camera to a large format camera like Ansel Adams used. I was one of a handful of women using this type of equipment. I wanted to see my subjects in minute detail.

I invested in several cameras and lenses, 8 x 10-inch film and imported photo papers. We built an addition on the house for my dedicated darkroom where, undisturbed, I could process my own black and white film.

Photography became my spiritual path. When out photographing in the countryside or developing prints in the darkroom, I felt like a different person. There is a creative zone in my head where I focused on only what was in front of me.

Setting up the large camera on its four-foot-high tripod took fifteen minutes. Everything about it is manual, and I had to make decisions every step. What made me stop to photograph? What lens will I use and what exposure? I slid the film holder in, put the dark cloth over my head, adjusted the focus, and prepared to take the shot.

Back in my darkroom, surrounded by darkness, and focused on the task, I carefully unloaded each sheet of film and eased it into the developer. The silence gave me a chance to think—or not. Working intently for hours, striving for that perfect print became my meditative practice. For the first time I believed that my long search had ended. I loved being in that creative zone, my spiritual path developing as I worked with beauty.

In the glow of the red safelight, with the timers ticking and the swishing of pungent chemistry in the trays, I wondered where this would take me. Was this my next career? Was my work good enough to share with others? Why and how would I do that? Would I ever find what I was looking for in life?

Eventually I took courses, attended conferences, learned to create platinum prints, became skilled at archival framing and matting, set up a website, then entered into the local art scene. You do see my continuing quest for perfectionism, don't you?

At shows and studio tours, I explained my choice of this unusual camera, the use of film rather than digital, demonstrated how prints are made, and ignored that little voice inside that said,

"You don't know what you're talking about. You aren't a real photographer."

More important than all of that was something more subtle. By mastering the technical aspects of this process, I was able to visually share my feelings in a way my words could not yet express.

I assumed this was to be my life going forward. When I was out photographing and producing beautiful images, I felt fulfilled, connected to my creative self. I looked at life through a 600mm lens, close up and personal. I was content until the beauty of life was obscured once again when my husband had a mild stroke.

For weeks, Stroke Team workers visited regularly to help his rehabilitation. Each therapist's visit involved an interview and suggestions or exercises. Life revolved around these appointments. The physical impairment was mild. More importantly, there had to be changes in our attitudes, our patience, and our expectations of each other. We faced the challenges of new routines and began to live with the realization there could be future strokes. I scaled back my photography.

By mastering the technical aspects of this process, I was able to visually share my feelings in a way my words could not yet express.

COPING WITH LIFE

The effects of this stress surfaced at unexpected moments and occasionally surprises me still. I realize how little attention I had paid to my own declining physical and emotional health while continuing to put others needs before my own out of habit. I did my best to avoid stressors I was aware of, but once in a while anxiety and fears were triggered.

Repeatedly, predictably, I reacted in the same way to some similar situations. Certain types of news always made me angry, sad, or frustrated. The mention of particular events or names could provoke a predictable response—I knew which ones would set me off. I would say, "If the news is all about politics, I don't want to watch."

It's as if the negative emotions were constantly triggered because my emotions are who I really am, and there was no changing that.

Why is it important to deal with these issues? You may be starting to see that, left unresolved, these negative emotions and fears may grow out of control later. What should make you sad for twenty minutes can take over your life. Anger makes people say and do things they regret and can cause illness.

There is much research now proving that our emotions affect our health and that memories of our life are stored in the unconscious mind. When those memories surface, the body experiences the same physical response as it did originally.

A quick internet search will provide you with videos and articles. It has taken time for this information to become accepted into our knowledge base, but it has been available for decades.

Over my career, I observed and participated in a wide range of interactions with adults, children, and groups of children together. I learned that young children act out, not because they are "bad" but for many other reasons that are not obvious to adults because we don't understand how children see the world.

If I hadn't felt the need to constantly prove myself as a child, perhaps I would not have gone down in flames, burning out. I am not looking to place blame. Although this is not my fault, I am the one who needs to deal with the emotions.

· CHAPTER 6 ·

My Ah-Ha Moment

Several years ago, life seemed smooth, just the way I imagined it should be. My husband and I had been married a long time. We traveled, skied, sailed, spent time with family. We were healthy and comfortable.

After a good friend of his died, he changed. He was at loose ends. He didn't enjoy being by himself. He wanted to know when I'd return from my photography shoot. Suddenly I felt like I was on a schedule, and that limited my creativity.

I sought refuge in my darkroom. Immersed in total darkness, not even the red safelight on, it is like a meditation room where I can be in the zone, undisturbed. It is silent, peaceful; time is irrelevant. Lost in my work and thoughts, the loud knock on the door startled me.

"Are you coming out of there soon? You've been in there all day."

"I'm in the middle of something. I have film in the fixer. I can't stop now."

"When do you want to have dinner?"

"When I am done here."

"Do you want me to start dinner now?"

"Well, I don't know how long I will be."

"Should I put the barbecue on now?"

Sighing loudly, "I'll be out in a half-hour."

Then, feeling guilty, I rushed to clean up, ending my work on a sour note, feeling that the last images were wasted.

I was short tempered for the rest of the evening, slamming pots and pans. I was angry at myself for being so annoyed with him. I was impatient with my impatience. I had a tough choice to make. I could let my spiritual path in the darkroom be derailed to accommodate his needs, or I could try to accommodate both of us. I was tired of feeling that I was the one to give in, yet I couldn't change anyone but myself. There must be another option.

Similar scenes began to happen more frequently. I was aggravated by this. My husband had no idea anything was wrong. Up until this time, we had honored each other's time in our creative spaces. But I had an art show coming up and work to do—printing in the darkroom, mounting, matting and framing—all of which demanded close attention to detail for uninterrupted periods of time.

There was no easy answer. I knew I was being petty and self-centered. I began to resent the time we spent in the evening together watching TV when I had other tasks to do. My attitude spilled over into other parts of our life. I felt like a Grinch.

From my point of view, the relationship further deteriorated. I became prickly and defensive. Rather than argue, I would leave the room imagining all kinds of revenge.

In a leap of faith, I trusted a friend's recommendation and made an appointment for a session with a woman who could remove negative emotions—whatever that meant. I love the synchronistic timing of events.

There was nothing to lose. I didn't fully understand what this session would do, but I was willing to find out, especially after being so angry with my husband.

· CHAPTER 7 ·

Meet the F.I.X. Code Founders

My initial experience with the F.I.X. Code was like magic.

Daniel Flear created the F.I.X. Code technique after his own epiphany. He describes the F.I.X. Code as a metaphorical device that allows us to communicate with the unconscious mind and make changes in the body.

F.I.X. Code stands for Flear Intuitive Extraction. *Code is an emotion.* It is the word you use to describe how you feel about the biggest problem you have in your life. If your emotion is "angry," that is the code word. If it is "hurt, sad, betrayed" or "this makes me sick," that is the code you work with and that is what disappears.

Clients call him "the Anxiety Whisperer." His work has repeatedly shown that we are not our emotions. This is a contradiction of mainstream belief. If you accept this new paradigm, it will change your world, how you think and feel about everything.

Daniel has a background in NLP, hypnosis, metaprograms, and

spiritual healing. He has studied with many of the originators of these techniques, such as Tony Robbins and Richard Bandler, the creator of NLP.

Daniel used his new method on friends and their friends, teenagers, and even strangers who were referred to him, with great success. He began to use this method with people who had tried other modalities to heal or who practiced other modalities and wanted another one in their tool kit.

Clients described the results, "I wish I'd found this years ago. I wouldn't have wasted all that time." They went away often forgetting they'd ever had a problem. If their issue was anger, they could be angry for an appropriate length of time. They were not angry days later, nor were they focused on the event that triggered that feeling.

When Daniel met them years later, the feelings attached to that emotion had not come back. It's possible that traditional methodology can do that, but from my own experience, it usually involves more than a fifteen-minute session.

Stacey K. Nye is the vice president of Ancient Gene Technologies. After experiencing one session with Daniel to remove *sad*, she knew she wanted to share this technique with the world. Stacey set out to learn all she could from Daniel and became an expert practitioner. She examined this method, teased it apart, and asked thousands of questions about the how and why it worked. She became the crash test dummy for investigating how this could be taught easily to others—either online or in private sessions.

This path in life chose Stacey. Until she met Daniel Flear, she had been involved in planning Olympic and the Commonwealth Games as well as G-8 and G-20 conferences and did classified work for several Prime Ministers and Presidents in North America. An athlete herself, she had grown up in a home that valued excellence and hard work. Writing and designing the F.I.X. Code online training course was a labor of love for her.

You can read more about them at thefixcode.com or their own websites.

The F.I.X. Code is unique.

Every experience in my life had led me to this point. Despite the difficulties, I do accept and embrace them all as they have shaped my life. Perhaps some of this will resonate with you or even be your wake-up call. Becoming a more conscious person has taken a lifetime so far and I am still working on it.

With the F.I.X. Code technique, there is no need for a backstory about the problem, no need to tell all the details of your hurt, guilt, or sadness. Once the emotion is gone, life changes. Imagine no longer feeling angry or guilty and being able to think clearly and rationally.

This is an experience and at the same time, a metaphorical device. Although I cannot fully explain how the F.I.X. Code works, what I can tell you is that it *does* work. It is non-invasive, simple, and fast. Because the details of the story aren't necessary, the client won't feel like they've said too much or revealed embarrassing events. When the session is over, the feelings attached to the memory that made the person feel guilty, sad, or betrayed are gone.

With the feelings attached to that memory gone, there is no need for the stories to come up. In the training course, Stacey explains that a person's sad stories are like pearls on a necklace. The feeling of *sad* is the string holding the necklace together. When a person feels sad, they feel all the sad stories because the stories were linked by the string of the necklace. A F.I.X. Code session removes the string, which is the feeling of *sad holding the necklace of stories together*. The pearls fall to the floor, no longer connected. Each pearl is simply a memory now without the sad attached. The great sadness the person felt at age eight when their parents divorced doesn't run them at age fifty.

With the feelings attached to that memory gone, there is no need for the stories to come up.

When I was putting my life back together, I spent a great deal of time working in my flower gardens, digging and planting. I cannot tell you how many times strangers would stop to talk. They told me stories about being ill, sad, or lonely.

We attract people who feel similar to us. I still work in my gardens, and people still stop to talk but the conversation is generally about the garden, beautiful flowers, and weather.

I like to think this is due to the F.I.X. Code changing my attitude so I no longer attract those people who are in such pain. My first experience with the F.I.X. Code changed my life and my relationship with my husband. It was simple and successful. I want to share it with you.

· CHAPTER 8 ·

I Meet Stacey Nye

I knocked on the door. Stacey answered, smiling and welcoming me to my first session of what would eventually be called the F.I.X. Code. Dressed in a sweater and jeans, she looked quite ordinary. What had I expected?

I took a deep breath and stepped forward. Once inside, I was committed to the session. I never enjoy telling my life story to strangers. As I wondered how to begin, Stacey offered tea.

That gave me a chance to relax and chat. I was to close my eyes and listen to her voice. There would be no probing into my life issues, my needs, goals, childhood fears. This seemed straightforward.

At that moment she asked, "What is the biggest problem in your life right now? And when you think about it, how does it make you feel?"

I had expected to say I felt angry but that wasn't quite right. I took a deep breath and checked inside. A picture formed in my mind, and I was able to put that feeling into words.

"Guilty."

Without missing a beat, Stacey asked, "Would it be okay if you didn't feel guilty anymore?"

When I said yes, she began.

I closed my eyes. As she guided me in letting go of that guilt, I was aware of everything around me. Once the visualization was done, she asked if I could think of a time in my past when I felt guilty.

I could think of many times when I had been guilty, but I realized the feeling of guilt was gone. I had to say, "No." Although that sounds unusual, I can't explain it. This had been unlike any intervention I had ever had. I left feeling lighthearted, as though a weight had been lifted.

The biggest surprise was that evening. I could feel compassion for how my husband was experiencing the loss of a dear friend. I was sorry for my behavior but wasn't feeling guilty. I was able to apologize without offering excuses. Our relationship took a definite turn for the better. I prioritized tasks for my upcoming show, set up a darkroom schedule, and ran this by my husband.

Because I was not fussing about being interrupted, I wasn't. The work went smoothly. My evenings were free to spend with him. If my husband knocked on the darkroom door, it didn't bother me, but he seldom interrupted after that. Because my reaction to him had changed, his behavior also changed.

Did You Have a Face Lift?

I was excited to tell friends and family about this new way of dealing with anger and fears, but people are often hesitant to try something new. I had to allow them to see my changes before they could consider that this worked. They would try this if and when they were ready. It was up to me to change my side of the relationship equation. The F.I.X. Code allowed that to happen.

After my first F.I.X. Code session with Stacey, all my guilt was gone, not just feeling guilty about my husband. I never gave *guilt* another thought. I couldn't even remember why I needed to see Stacey. Can you imagine not feeling guilty about anything? I came to realize that I couldn't predict or control how others felt about me. I stopped feeling guilty that I hadn't been able make my Mom's pain disappear or make my husband feel less grief about the loss of his friend.

After my first F.I.X. Code session with Stacey, all my guilt was gone.

The F.I.X. Code session with Stacey was simple. The problem of being interrupted in the darkroom made me feel guilty. This guilty feeling had been with me for a lifetime. It is personal. The same scenario may not bother anyone else

That feeling of "*guilty*" was the code we worked with. After the session, I recalled events that caused that guilt but not the feeling of guilt. This was like my "guilty pearl necklace." There were many stories on the guilty necklace. The guilt that had kept me frustrated and feeling somehow indebted to others was gone. It has been gone for five years. I call that success!

After my first session, I asked, "What do I need to do now?"

"Look for the good! It is everywhere."

That became my new mantra.

Within a month, I couldn't remember my reason for seeing

Stacey. The session receded into the background. The session had worked. Life was back on track!

It's hard to believe this can happen so easily unless you have experienced a session. Whatever your version of the sad story of your life might be, it starts to change. You will tell it if you must, but the emotional charge is gone. It's simply a story, much like I have told you about my life-long guilt. Remember my frustration? I can smile at that now.

Over the next year there were noticeable changes in me that puzzled friends.

"Do you have a new haircut?"

"You look so rested."

"What's your secret?"

"Have you had a facelift?"

The answer was that those codes (emotions), the negative emotions and fears had kept me in detrimental behavior patterns. The worry, guilt, anger, sadness, and fears show in our posture, expressions and language although we may not be aware.

Their questions led me to realize that the sad look, the frown lines, the sighing had disappeared along with the emotions they were attached to. I was ecstatic. I felt different, and it showed.

It is not up to me to convince anyone to try the F.I.X. Code. I believe people who are ready will find this. Statistics show that mental health issues are increasing. This is a simple solution for anxiety, fears, and other emotions. This can change lives, and I am pleased to spread the news.

· CHAPTER 9 ·

The F.I.X. Code Is Not...

It is NOT hypnosis, NLP, talk therapy, Reiki, EFT, Cognitive Behavior Therapy, Behavior Modification, counseling, psychotherapy, biofeedback, exposure therapy, energy work, dream therapies, mindfulness, shamanism, relaxation, yoga, meditation, tai chi, or a combination of diet and exercise. If there is anything I missed, it likely isn't that either.

These are all wonderful tools as we move toward becoming more conscious beings. Practitioners from different modalities have taken the F.I.X. Code training and commented, "The F.I.X. Code is the real thing."

I personally needed something more effective than all the techniques I'd tried in the past. I love that the F.I.X. Code works, is very practical, and doesn't require any props. A session can be done anywhere—in a restaurant or in the car—and it works.

Does that mean the F.I.X. Code is something new?

YES.

In my first session, there was no discussion about my problem. I answered one question about my feelings, and the process began. It took fifteen minutes, and it worked. It was simple.

Let me repeat that.

I answered one question, listened to the instructions, and visualized. The feeling went away and did not come back.

The F.I.X. Code allows people to stop replaying memories over and over. This is more important than I first understood.

Stacey's Sad is Gone

Let me explain a bit more about how the F.I.X. Code developed. About ten years ago, Daniel Flear used this technique with a group of women wanting to eliminate some emotional baggage. One of the women, Stacey Nye, had spent years trying to heal her life. She was desperate.

After Daniel used the F.I.X. Code to successfully remove the feeling of "*sad,*" Stacey announced that she was going to learn to do this and share the technique with the world. They formed a business partnership.

As a mom, Stacey knew if other mothers could learn this, the next generation could change. She realized the huge impact this could have on the world. Imagine teens who were no longer ruled by hurt and betrayal, sad, or angry. Life would be different. She has used this technique successfully with her son to navigate him through adolescence. The usual issues that teens face have been diffused gracefully, without arguments and rebellion.

Because she wanted to be able to share this easily, she pushed it to the limit, becoming an expert and training other practitioners.

She has done sessions on the phone, in person, and in the bleachers at a ballgame. One advantage is the lack of accessories.

I am not trying to diagnose or advise you, simply recounting my experience with this technique. A client does not tell their life story, details of the problem, or any history. When they answer how they feel about the biggest problem in life, that feeling is the code the practitioner works with. The clients close their eyes, listen to the instructions, and visualize. In the end, the negative feeling, anxiety, or fear is gone and does not come back.

It is that simple.

· CHAPTER 10 ·

Why the F.I.X. Code is Different

The F.I.X. Code Technique is *the way to achieve what all those self-help books advise us to do.*

The F.I.X. Code Technique *is* the way to achieve what all those self-help books advise us to do. This deceptively simple technique is a quantum leap forward in healing. It works and it lasts. We know that our emotional state affects our physical body both negatively and positively. Consider that those negative emotions you carry around might be making you ill. That could be a compelling reason to change those feelings.

Unlike other techniques, this technique doesn't mask problems or work only for a short time. There are no gadgets, chants, dances, or ceremonies. It can be done anywhere, with anyone who is in need. Anyone can learn to do this.

One of the books I had read was the *Power of Now* by Eckhart Tolle. It seemed to have the answers for a life of joy and magic. I embraced the concepts whole heartedly. I believed I could find a way to live in a state of presence and to be grateful, as he had. His life sounded so unencumbered.

I did not want to take myself so seriously, but I had been raised to be overly responsible, and life was serious stuff. I wanted to slow down and let the problems pass. I believed Tolle when he said that the fears and sadness are not mine, and they will come and go.

But they never seemed to go and stay away. I had no idea how to just be, how to stop resisting, and how to be grateful as he proposed. This all sounded amazing, but when I tried, it never lasted. I couldn't force the feelings nor make them stay.

When I burned out, being grateful was not on my radar. The concept meant nothing to me as I tried to simply exist. You have already seen the list of how I tried unsuccessfully to find that elusive presence.

I continued my search wondering if I'd ever find a solution.

Searching for Epiphany

What have I discovered since then? For one, Eckhart Tolle talks about his epiphany when he discovered an intuitive answer to who he was. He then spent two years sitting on a park bench in intense joy.

I have never had such an epiphany. I had never found intense joy or an intuitive answer to my questions about life that made me want to sit on a park bench as he did. Without a spontaneous epiphany, I could not begin to replicate Tolle's experience for myself, but I have found my own version.

The F.I.X. Code Technique allowed me to clear out all the negative chatter and hang ups that stood between me and that intense joy. For me, the results are like the results of Tolle's epiphany. The F.I.X. Code is as close as possible to my spontaneous epiphany. It has given me the gift of being able to live in a state of presence.

When people advise me to "change my circumstances, suck it up, just do the work" with whatever life has given me, the missing link is the *how*. *How* can I do that?

> *When people advise me to "change my circumstances, suck it up, just do the work" with whatever life has given me, the missing link is the how.*

The F.I.X. Code *is* the *how* you do this. It *is* how you clear your head so you can think, take advice, understand options and consequences. Life is about choices. We are in this moment because of choices made long before now. That is not easy to accept when one feels burdened, burned out, or victimized.

People are advised to take responsibility for their lives, choices and their path. But *how* does one do that? That part of the equation is of utmost importance. It was missing. When I read all those books seeking answers, I noticed the sage advice was based on the personal experiences of the writers.

But I am not one of them. Life has not lined up in the same way for me as it did for each of the gurus or anyone else in the world.

If I'm not able to replicate their experience, I should not expect the same results. Why would I? I am not the same person they are. It follows that I'm not going to be successful in the exact same way. The books became an inspiration but never a solution.

The F.I.X. Code Technique does not need me to do any of the above. I don't need to do anything. I don't need a road map of how to pray, meditate, open my heart the same way. I don't need or want to have a 200-page manual on where to place my healing hands or how to raise my vibrational level.

The benefits that Eckhart Tolle writes about that other spiritual advisers also define are available to me after my F.I.X. Code sessions. Those many authors were espousing the same concept but it was never going to be available to me. It would not matter how many of their books I read. It really is easy to understand now that I know what was missing and how it can be accessed.

Intellectually I understood what they wrote about but I wasn't able to truly comprehend. Much of their advice now makes sense and can be achieved because I have a way to clear the blocks. The F.I.X. Code replicates their epiphanies or visions. My vibrational level increases when I have those negative emotions removed by using the F.I.X. Code.

My vibrational level increases when I have those negative emotions removed by using the F.I.X. Code.

No doubt you love whatever technique you are currently involved with. Awesome. If you are committed to it and it gives you one hundred percent success, stay with it. If change isn't an option, stay on your current path.

THE F.I.X. CODE

But if you are frustrated for any reason—with lack of progress, road blocks, weekly counseling sessions or feeling that your problems are never ending, if you long for a way to replicate the elusive epiphany—then read further.

The wonderful difference about the F.I.X. Code is that you don't have to align your life events with anyone else's to experience the healing you seek and deserve. It is about you. Your feelings, your emotion—that is your code to healing.

If you feel that you are not the problem but don't know what is, you're in the right place to find out. I'm pleased that you have arrived here.

Your feelings, your emotion—
that is your code to healing.

· CHAPTER 11 ·

Cover Stories

A well-designed book cover will catch your attention—the image, colors and layout work together to hint at the narrative inside. We pick up the book and read. If the cover doesn't appeal, we may miss a good tale.

This can also be true of the way people present themselves to the world. I call this a cover story. People can spend time, energy, and money to create their image. Smiles block fears, fashions distract, possessions impress, and people hide behind their career. They present a secure, confident cover story to the world while inside doubts and fears, conflicts, and heartbreak may be a few of the emotions running their lives.

It happens all the time. We see what people choose to show us. We interpret this through our own filters and label them—happy, aggressive, sad, kind and more. Inside, a person may be angry at the challenges they face, hurt by others, or wanting to retaliate.

They may feel powerless or guilt ridden. Few would suspect what is going on inside another person's mind.

A cover story hides insecurities and inner beauty. We are pressured by advertising to conform, to look and be our best, but our reasons for doing this are personal. There are hundreds of fears that people conceal and just as many talents.

If you are one of the people ready to make a change, then come with me. Match your cover story to the real you. Find that inner peace. There is a reason you have picked up a book about how to be healed.

You Are Not Your Emotions

There are people that can be described as angry, sad, or anxious, and they believe it is impossible to change. They are defined by their emotions.

The concept that we are our emotions been a long-accepted belief. It is difficult to change an established belief and much harder to change one that is widely held by society. When people find support for their beliefs, they defend their choices by investing time, money, skill, and may establish a community of like-minded people. We label and slot ourselves into categories as if that tells people who we really are.

The F.I.X. Code Technique reinforces that we are not our emotions.

The F.I.X. Code Technique reinforces that we are not our emotions.

Emotions can be changed to allow people to work toward greater consciousness and a chance to live in presence. The emotion does not define them. That is a huge step in changing a belief system. It is a paradigm shift from believing they are their emotions to knowing that their emotional reaction to life can change easily.

Reflect for a Moment

Have you ever felt unexplained anger that seemed out of proportion to the problem?

Have you ever witnessed a four-year-old yell at mom, "I hate you," and wondered how she would know that phrase?

Are you sad? Is there any joy in your life?

Do you have difficulty saying no to requests from others and then feel taken advantage of when they don't show appreciation?

Do you believe people only call when they want something from you?

Do you give your time and service to others at the expense of your own well-being?

Do you have difficulty making decisions about everyday events—changing your mind in case there is a better choice?

Do you avoid social functions or public places because you are embarrassed to be seen or afraid to meet people you know?

Are goodbyes difficult?

Are you a workaholic, compulsive about tidiness, or addicted to making money?

Do you eat, drink, or use drugs to change your emotional state?

Are you unable to make difficult decisions?

Are you making pictures of your future going wrong?

Did you have an ah-ha moment, answer yes, or feel uneasy

about any of these?

People may not be aware of what shaped their behaviors. Each of the above is a clue to an emotional state. The triggers—sounds, smells, objects, tastes, or feelings may appear unrelated. The behavior is not random. With the F.I.X. Code it is not necessary to know—it is irrelevant.

This book is a personal compilation of my experiences with a new healing modality called the F.I.X. Code Technique. This is not meant to diagnose or advise, nor is it a research paper. Some examples are my own or stories from conversations. Others are examples from people I worked with. Names and circumstances have been changed.

I'd like to describe how this random selection of *"codes"* appears in life and a few ways that people unconsciously deal with these emotions.

Keeping Anger at All Costs

Sylvia and I were at the coffee shop catching up when she launched word for word into a story that she had told me many times—exactly the same tone of voice, same words, same facial expression, same body language. It was like a video loop.

"At the party Saturday, I was telling Jeanine about our trip when she started talking to someone beside her. She turned away as if I wasn't there. Why do I bother? She never changes."

"How does that make you feel?"

"Invisible. I hate that!"

When someone repeatedly tells a story verbatim with the same amount of energy and emotion attached to it, it is a clue that their emotions are running them. Have you ever listened to a friend tell an old story with the same detail and intense emotion as if it had happened just recently?

It was tempting to commiserate with Sylvia as I had done previously, but that would anchor in her feelings. Yet I wanted to be supportive. I was able to remain detached and listen to her story as she continued to vent. The person she spoke about had never treated me in the same way, so I was able to remain objective. Because this code is about Sylvia's emotions, it didn't affect me the same way.

When she had finished, I asked Sylvia to think about how she felt about the biggest problem in her life right now, knowing that it might not have been what she was venting about.

She promptly responded, "Angry."

A F.I.X. Code practitioner would ask Sylvia the Magic Question, then have her close her eyes and listen to the instructions. The process would take about fifteen minutes and when it was over, Sylvia wouldn't be able to find that level of anger in herself over that event or other similar events.

She might even forget that this had bothered her. In future, when a similar interruption happens, Sylvia would handle this very differently. She could ignore the interruption, walk away, point out that she had been interrupted, or many other possible options.

But that is not what will happen. Sylvia maintains that her life is perfect so won't try the F.I.X. Code, yet there are signs that her emotions and habits are affecting her health and her life. She is not willing to change her behavior and therefore, her life.

A therapist might ask probing questions about Sylvia's childhood, her relationship with her parents and siblings, the family history, personality traits she had inherited, and more. It would be interesting to analyze. It could also take weeks of sessions. Sylvia might discover the underlying reason for her anger, the therapist would have case notes, and Sylvia might be prescribed some form of medication or ongoing treatment.

For now, Sylvia will continue to be interrupted, spoken over, ignored at times, and react the same way with the same amount of anger. At any time, she might decide she can let go of that anger, or she can let herself be defined by it. This story she tells is not the only indication of anger in her life. It shows up in her language, her tone of voice, her forceful responses to people, and a know-it-all attitude when she corrects other people in conversation. She has already had health concerns.

The issue right now is that Sylvia repeatedly reacts the same way. When she reacts this way, the force of her emotions is like a tsunami for people nearby. People don't appreciate this energy, and I have been told that some people avoid her for this reason.

The cover story she believes she presents to the world is disconnected from her inner reality. If this is to change, Sylvia needs to deal with her emotional responses.

· CHAPTER 12 ·

Emotions Can Be Changed

The F.I.X. Code removes the emotional charge from the event, allowing the memory to become a story that may be forgotten soon after. This means that emotions can be changed and do not need to define a person.

The emotions evoked are attached to deeply-embedded memories. The memory triggers the emotional response. The emotions are the way people have been programmed throughout life to respond. The emotion attached to those memories can be easily removed so that the response to the memory changes and along with that, so does their behavior. Life changes.

The response to the memory changes and along with that, so does their behavior. Life changes.

The F.I.X. Code is a way to remove these negative emotions and fears that have been instilled long ago. There is a choice: remain in the same emotional pattern as Sylvia did or change the emotional response to those memories, changing life, just as my *"guilty"* response to being interrupted in the darkroom changed.

It is possible and easily done. Everyone I know has emotions that run their lives, at times making them miserable, feeling out of control, overwhelmed, or angry. But many of them will not risk changing their emotional responses. They say, "My life is perfect." Another friend explained, "I am afraid to begin this. I don't know where it will lead."

Ignoring opportunities because of fear or mistrust illustrates how fear can run a life. No one knows how life will unfold, and a change could be positive. Fear is a choice, but many people fear change. Eliminating these fears and being open to other possibilities is a chance to take the road less traveled.

Living with the stress generated by these negative emotions can lead to health issues. Common stress indicators are sleep problems, asthma, obesity, heart problems, diabetes, depression, gastrointestinal problems, and possibly dementia, according to WebMD.

Living with the stress generated by these negative emotions can lead to health issues.

When Daniel Flear first created this technique, he had his own epiphany that allowed him to see that we are not our emotions. He explains the F.I.X. Code Technique as a metaphorical device used to remove negative emotions and fears from the unconscious mind. These emotions and fears are attached to your memories. The unconscious mind brings up the memories that trigger the fears and emotions.

When I first heard about this technique, I was intrigued by what it meant to have negative emotions removed. I had no idea how this would impact my life. I didn't need to know how it worked. That information came later.

Fears and Anxieties

Fears are personal. In our minds, we make images of the future going wrong. This creates a fear or anxiety about the future. Fears are not facts. When we make choices based on fear, it keeps us small. Of all the things we worry about going wrong, how many ever actually happen?

Perhaps you are handling fears or anxiety right now. What you are doing may be working for you or maybe not. Perhaps you are progressing slowly with regular counseling sessions. Perhaps you don't like taking medications.

From my reading, it seems that many people believe they are powerless over anxiety or fears. Attempting to heal, they get locked into support groups or regular therapy sessions. Sometimes this becomes their social life as they believe that only people in these groups understand them.

Because of the complex relationship between emotions, mental illness, and substance abuse, treatment is not a simple process. Daniel has used the F.I.X. Code with addicts, but it is beyond the scope of my understanding and knowledge.

It is possible to heal in a new way without having to share the details of the hurt and anger. Take back life. Wouldn't it be wonderful to experience emotions in the moment for an appropriate length of time, not forever? Imagine being able to think clearly, make rational decisions, or not be drawn into anyone else's crisis.

My life changed in obvious ways immediately. I was able to change stressful habits. I no longer felt compelled to solve problems that others brought to my attention. Everyone needs the freedom to experience life on their own terms.

Update your beliefs. Change those emotions. Live the life you create.

Update your beliefs.
Change those emotions.
Live the life you create.

Part Two

"No man is an island, entire of itself."
— John Donne

Life is about relationship. By now, I hope you have made the connection that your emotions affect your behavior and therefore your relationships even if you are not aware of this.

People have many choices in life. Some wish to become aware of their emotions and behavior and how this affects their relationships, others do not. Consider the possibility that the consequences of behavior travel further than people anticipate.

The "butterfly effect" is used to illustrate how small changes can have a large impact on the behavior of people with whom you interact. If, like Sylvia, people are angry and unwittingly upset others or themselves, imagine how eliminating this unconscious emotion of anger could change her interactions with others. They, in turn, modify their own behavior that could further influence the behavior of more people. The changes can continue exponentially.

From my own experience, I have seen this in action. After my first F.I.X. Code session, I sat in my car thinking about the past hour. A monarch butterfly settled on my windshield briefly before flying away. I love the symbolism of this. My behavior changed effortlessly after that session. I witnessed the reaction of people around me when they felt my changes. I saw and heard them alter their own behavior. How far did this travel? I imagine it just kept going. The F.I.X. Code has already changed the world.

The F.I.X. Code has already changed the world.

In the next chapters, you will follow real stories about hurt, fear, and anger to discover what this looks like and how life changes without anxiety and sadness. When people are being unconsciously run by emotions, they are not aware of how it affects their lives. They think it is just the way they are—it's their personality—but that is an outdated belief. The F.I.X. Code will change life quickly and easily.

· CHAPTER 13 ·

As We Grow

NO FILTERS FROM BIRTH TO SEVEN

No one truly knows your life story. Do we know our own? We judge, we compare, we praise or denigrate ourselves. We want to do better, be better, and we try.

We strive to be as good as we possible. We shouldn't blame ourselves if we fall short of our expectations; however, we are responsible for our decisions and choices in life. In the training, when Daniel and Stacey teach the science behind the method, you'll understand why it is not my fault. I accept that I am responsible for my decisions, and I am not looking to blame for my past. I want to explain without giving you a course!

All my life, I have been longing to find my purpose. The search began when I was very young. I asked many questions. I was a challenging child, and children know when answers don't ring true.

Taught not to argue with adults—reinforced by the "children should be seen and not heard" theory—the confusion, frustration, and hurt feelings were hidden away for years. I would never have believed I felt this way.

Most children have fears, which they label as the boogey man or a monster under the bed. Mine were the imaginary lion.

My behavior was influenced when I misinterpreted events around me. I observed and tried to make sense of what I saw, heard, felt. My parents didn't explain the rationale of their adult decisions to anyone as I have seen some parents currently doing. I trusted them.

Often, I could not live up to what I believed the adults expected of me. Adults forget that children view the world differently, think differently, and interpret their surroundings as a child, not as an adult does.

I was headstrong, independent, curious. My favorite retort, "You are not the boss of me," explains so much of my attitude throughout life. I must have challenged and frustrated my parents. They threatened to send me to boarding school so someone else could deal with me. When scolded, I felt confused because it was not always clear to me what I had done wrong. I was a good student, but only a perfect test score good enough for my father—that became my standard of measurement.

Adult Body—Childlike Emotions

All those childish feelings were buried deep inside. They may be labeled as rebellion, perfectionism, bossy behavior, over achieving, confrontational, hurtful retaliation. On the other hand, I was also technical, artistic, quick thinking, and athletic.

I'm sure my parents thought I was a difficult child. I wanted to know how and why things worked but soon learned not to ask so many questions. My teenage years were pretty typical: rebellious and emotional. I managed to chronologically become an adult, but it was another twenty years before I began to understand my journey.

There was my cover story—the person who wanted to shine and be a star, the understanding, fun and compassionate friend, the loyal partner, and the loving daughter. There was also the hidden me with doubts, fears, anxieties—the second guessing myself, the insecurities, frustrations and lack of patience, the feelings of not being good enough, the unfairness of being the eldest.

I had become aware that adults weren't as all-knowing as I had believed. But it was years before I understood that parents do their best with whatever skills they have. We parent as we were parented and our parents were parented. It takes a great deal of effort to change those values and patterns. Parenting is a challenging role in life, and I wonder how prepared anyone could be.

Truly Growing Up

Have you ever felt an emotion but tried to hide the feeling? Oh, the energy it takes to be something you really are not. It's tiring to live a lie, never being able to relax and admit your worst fears, not even to yourself.

I was constantly defending myself to my inner critic, trying to convince myself that I was a good person. My spiritual teacher told me that it was not enough to be a good person. I trusted her and accepted that being better than good was worth pursuing. I tried to go the extra mile, spread the joy, be more than helpful. Whatever I might have done naturally, I tried to augment.

If I was making a donation to a charity, I gave more than my budget allowed. I gave my time freely to volunteer after work, which then meant I was rushed to do my own chores. I over delivered on projects. If taking food to a bereaved friend, it was prepared from scratch—and I am not an enthusiastic cook. This added to my stress level but didn't stop me.

I played right into my overcompensating behavior. The more I did that, the more I felt it was what I had to do until I started to resent being there for everyone else.

Through sessions with the FIX Code technique. I discovered that many of these misconceptions, beliefs, fears, and anxieties had their origin years ago. I had no idea that they ran my life. I began to mature when I realized that there were other forces at work besides my own will.

Does that resonate with you?

· CHAPTER 14 ·

Fears and Anxiety

Joanne's Piano

Joanne and I are lounging in the shade one day, catching up on the news. She has been telling me about her volunteer work playing piano for the seniors at the local nursing home. They loved those afternoons—the songs she played brought back memories.

"I'm thinking about selling my piano."

"Really? Why?" Joanne is a gifted musician. Maybe her hands are sore or she's too busy with her volunteer work.

"Well, I am not going to live forever, and I don't want the kids to have to sell the piano. They won't know what to do with it. They'll probably give it away."

Those words are like a dagger piercing my heart. What is she talking about? Her grand piano is the focal point in her living room, her pride and joy.

"But you love your music."

"Yes, but it's only a matter of time before I die. I've outlived my parents."

"Is there something you are not telling me?" This sounds serious.

"No, everything with my last checkup was fine."

This conversation blind-sided me. Joanne is a generation older than I am. Her concerns were valid as she's had serious medical issues in the past. I hated that she spoke so matter-of-factly. I tried to listen and honor her feelings.

In reality, this put a damper on any fun we might have had! When she called next time, I kept the call short but was not ready to see her again. Her comments were valid and so were my feelings. I was frustrated, not saddened, by her thoughts.

In the past, I had tried to reason with her, talk her out of this train of thought. It seemed like she was setting herself up to be a self-fulfilling prophecy. There could be many reasons for her comments, but I could only change my *own* behavior if we were to remain friends.

After my first F.I.X. Code session, I had begun to connect my symptoms and behavior to my feelings. This one felt like a fear.

I'm writing only about my own experiences and not trying to diagnose. If you feel any similarity to your own experiences, that is a coincidence.

I want to illustrate how my negative emotions and fears presented themselves to me, how I dealt with them after years of traditional therapy, before finally hoping they would disappear.

What Fear Looks and Feels Like

In my mind, there are momentary fears—before stepping onto

the stage to speak before a large crowd, the zip line stomach flops, or being startled by a loud noise.

There are other fears that present as many different forms of anxiety. It may be anxiety about leaving the house because of fear of being hurt. Anxiety begins as the person makes pictures of the future going wrong and feels a nervousness somewhere in their body. The anxiety keeps them home. If they do go for an appointment, that fear that something might go wrong makes them hurry home. There are many such fears.

There are also fears that become so deeply buried that they seem disconnected from the event. That is how Joanne's comment triggered my own fear.

Our piano conversation stayed with me all the next day. I had that nagging feeling that something needed to change. Joanne's words were only the trigger for my negative emotions and wouldn't have affected anyone else in the same way.

Something showed up. Can you guess the fear?

There are also fears that become so deeply buried that they seem disconnected from the event

---

F.I.X. CODE SESSION TWO

I arrived for my second F.I.X. Code session with a list of feelings and symptoms associated with my reaction to Joanne's comments. The list included frustrated, fed up, discouraged, worried, pointless, ineffective, aggravating, a waste of time, and energy sucking. When Stacey asked the Magic Question—how I felt about the biggest problem in my life right now—my response was that I was afraid, but not afraid of Joanne dying.

It was the *fear of saying goodbye*.

With the F.I.X. Code Technique, that fear was gone in fifteen minutes.

In a session, I never have to give details. This fear had been with me my whole life. To illustrate where it began, I will take a look back at it and show you how this trigger worked. It looked like fear of my friend dying, but that wasn't it.

To show you how events become triggers that appear unrelated to our emotions, I am going to trace the fear to my childhood. This is for explanation only. It is not part of a F.I.X. Code session.

Childhood Memories Become a Fear

Every summer my Mom, sister, and I flew across the country to visit my 65-year-old grandmother for two weeks. We had fun exploring the prairies, swimming, visiting, and taking trips to the mountains.

It was a magical time that I loved, yet I had distinct, puzzling memories of my grandmother standing at the window, waving goodbye, and crying as we left for the airport. Why?

My mother was sad—maybe she cried, too—but I didn't understand. No one explained. Sometimes I cried a bit. The sadness was contagious. The tears were puzzling.

I was excited about flying home to see my dad, the dog, my bike. Using my unfiltered child logic, I decided that Mom was afraid she wouldn't be able to visit again; she was sad because Grandma was old. If my mom was feeling like that, I should too—she is my role model. I hid how I felt and buried that feeling of confusion and sadness, fear and apprehension. I never really knew

Mom's feelings, but I will call it a fear.

I wasn't aware of this connection, but it made a huge impact on me—one that was repeated annually until Grandma died when I was twenty-two. This was the final goodbye.

By then, Mom's fear had expanded to include my leaving home. She made me promise to phone every time I arrived at my destination. For years, we had a phone code so she'd know I was safe. Let the phone ring twice, then hang up.

Eventually her fear became my fear. How that happens, I don't know. Before my mother was twenty years old, her father, a sister, and baby brother had died. The family knew the grief of loss and the final goodbye. This would have been part of the emotions they carried. Mom seldom spoke about this. I learned that we keep secrets, especially about our feelings.

Goodbyes have never been pleasant. There was always an undertone of sadness and fear that this was to be a final visit—even more intense if distance was involved. As a young child observing these events without explanation, I drew my own conclusions, and they became part of my hard wiring. I didn't have a clue they were running me until Joanne's comment triggered my reaction.

My Fear Is Gone

Having that fear of saying goodbye removed in a F.I.X. Code session changed my relationship with my friend. Joanne's comments didn't trigger those feelings anymore. When she brought up selling the piano, I could hear what she was really saying. My fears were no longer in the way. This connection may not make sense to you, but that is the thing about triggers—they are personal.

Several years later, Joanne still has her piano and continues to volunteer. We see each other often, but she has never again mentioned selling her piano. When I recently mentioned the piano, she spoke instead about her years of training.

An interesting note: with my fear removed I now see this fear in others. Once I found the trigger and the fear, it wasn't possible to ignore it or not see it. I am aware of the fear of saying goodbye in some people. It plays out in all kinds of ways, from little rituals to tears or stoicism and anything in between.

I continued to have F.I.X. Code sessions with Stacey as the need arose. Immediately the negative emotion was gone. I would contact her any time I felt a "code" come up.

Friends still wonder, "What is different about you?" Or comment, "Have you lost weight?" The change was about getting rid of those negative emotions and fears that kept me in old behavior patterns. The worry, guilt, anger, sadness, and fears were now gone. I was ecstatic!

· CHAPTER 15 ·

Fear of Financial Ruin

4 a.m. The clock glared at me.

Why am I awake? This is so unusual.

My mind sifts through the details of the past week. I am overwhelmed by a constant bombardment of stressful emotions that keep me circling the same issue. I am intensely annoyed by a series of events that my friend, Pat, has set in motion.

The trigger for this had been subtle and had nothing to do with my friend. I ordered a charging pad for my phone from an ad on social media. It didn't arrive as expected. Had I been scammed out of my money? I had promised myself last year after being scammed on Facebook that I'd never shop like that again, and yet I had ignored all my instincts. For days I expected this feeling of being scammed to disappear—but it has stayed and now wakened me as if to say, "Face me. Deal with me."

Wide-awake and puzzled, I examine the details of the event,

looking for clues, realizing I've done this many times already. Eventually I can identify the feeling attached to this. There it is! The feeling is "being taken advantage of."

Oh, that's a big one. But I'm pretty sure I have dealt with this before.

Knowing that, I dig deeper.

The feeling really has to do with lending my friend some money. Although it was to be repaid within weeks, after two years of waiting, I'm starting to *believe* I was foolish.

Money between friends and family has always been a tough call. It can break a relationship. It's high on the list of reasons partners fight. Knowing the circumstances of my friend's life, I had been happy to lend money the first time, and the second time, and the third time—you get the picture.

Stay with me as I dig deeper. It's still only 4:30 a.m. My language has changed as I describe this. It is no longer about a feeling. Now it is a *belief* that I was foolish to lend the money, to *believe* it would be repaid, to *believe* that I was more to this person than a metaphorical wallet opening on command.

And yet, at the same time as I feel taken advantage of, I realize I played a huge role in this because of my own belief system. This deeply hidden belief that I was foolish allowed me to lend money without really thinking the situation through. That was the obvious side of the problem.

If I ignore this feeling, it will *not* go away.

If I ignore this feeling, it will not *go away.*

The other side was that my friend needed something good to happen in order to move forward in life, and I had the means to provide that. Two years ago, I could support that. I could help. My worry had been triggered by the charging pad scam. It had me believing I was foolish with my money because the loan was still outstanding.

I can think of nothing else in the middle of the night. I am fortunate that there is a solution that will allow me to move forward, think clearly and outside the box. The F.I.X. Code Technique is at my fingertips.

I took the F.I.X. Code training four years ago, did my practice work with about a hundred clients, and continue to use this with friends. I could access the technique through my online course material and do this for myself, but I prefer to call Stacey in the morning.

It will take fifteen minutes to get rid of this emotional baggage.

Right now, it's still dark, and I am not quite finished with this belief.

TEASING THIS APART

This code was not part of my core value system but a *belief* that was attached to an emotion. It prevented me from thinking about anything other than this situation for the past week. The feeling hovered over my shoulder and popped up in a quiet moment. Because of this, I kept myself busier than usual and accomplished little. It really sapped my energy, fogged my brain, kept me from working.

I had been creating pictures in my mind of the future going wrong.

This belief that I was foolish is linked to a fear. Oh my! And here come the images of my future going wrong because of my foolishness. Can you imagine what they might be? Sure, you can, but I'll start you off. Fear of not being able to pay my bills...financial ruin...bankruptcy...not having enough...not having any...losing my home...and this spirals quickly out of control.

The actual numbers are irrelevant, as is the fact that I have a great life without the money being repaid. My imaginings are fears of my own making, not facts.

Do you see how my unconscious mind took over and controlled my thoughts?

The unique thing about the F.I.X. Code Technique is that I don't have to tell all these details, all the twists and turns of my mind. I identity the feeling attached to the biggest problem in my life, and the session begins.

It ends with my no longer having those feelings attached to the fear. The fear shrinks and I can deal with it rationally, logically, with a clear head. There are options and many ways to deal with this that do not include a panicky outlook and an attack on myself. The negative self-talk will go. The original problem will continue to exist but will not consume my life. I will deal with it and move on.

That is very different from how I had been looking at the problem all week. In fact, the whole problem seemed to disappear.

Fear of Financial Death

Financial death is a huge fear that many of us live with unconsciously. The fear is obvious in our language in comments like, "I'm afraid I'll lose my shirt."

"I need to save more money. I can't treat myself."

"I have to ask my husband for the money."

"I have to leave an estate for my children."

"I can't afford it."

Sometimes this fear stems from a time when money was tight, when there was a nationwide depression and the fear hung like a blanket over the nation. But even then, not everyone was affected, and there are few alive now who lived through the stock market crash in 1929. Yet that fear is present.

Remember that we are not to blame for these emotions and fears. This fear could have been passed down generations from those who did worry about feeding their families or losing their home in the depression. It would show up in their habits and passed on to children. We know it is possible pass on our tendencies for habits and fears through DNA.

The fear of financial death keeps people thinking small. It becomes a form of limiting punishment even when not necessary. It can masquerade as a habit of being frugal.

I live in a four seasons tourist area. There are people who have homes here for ski season or vacation. During winter and summer, the population increases tenfold. Housing prices are exorbitant. Most of the jobs are in the service industry with minimum pay. Affordable housing and good paying jobs are scarce.

There is a volunteer-run second-hand store that recycles clothing, designer label merchandise, household items, and toys. Proceeds go to support day care, food banks, and community outreach programs.

People who appear financially comfortable consistently shop there. There are always Mercedes-Benz or BMWs parked outside as people hunt for bargains inside.

The concept of the store was to provide affordable items for those who were in need. While there are many reasons, it is interesting that people who don't need to shop there, do. I believe fear of financial death is more common than we know. We can see and hear the language of that fear in everyday conversations.

The F.I.X. Code can get rid of that fear and let you see your way out of a difficult financial situation. My fear had begun when I was put into a slightly uncomfortable situation involving money. I could not think clearly about the situation. Once this became a conscious problem, in fear I blew it out of proportion.

What we think about and imagine often become real. If I continued to imagine this scenario leading to financial ruin, then it more than likely could come true.

The Fear Is Gone

The unconscious mind doesn't know that I don't want financial ruin. It only sees the pictures in my head or hears the words "financial ruin" and then sets about making those come true. It is why we must think positively, but that was impossible with the way my mind was racing.

The F.I.X. Code removed that fear. How I felt changed. I saw the situation without all the negative feelings that fear raised and relaxed knowing that Pat would pay me back when she could. I had helped a friend through a difficult time. My finances were fine.

Two days after my F.I.X. Code session removed that fear, the charging pad arrived!

· CHAPTER 16 ·

Anger

WHAT ANGER LOOKS AND FEELS LIKE

Stacey locked the door to her gym at 12:00 p.m. each day, rushed to her car, and headed off to do all the errands associated with her business. First stop was for cleaning supplies. While in the store, she picked up three t-shirts for work. After a quick stop for a slice of pizza and pop, she went into the bank to pay bills.

Out of the bank at 3:05 p.m., she drove to the far end of town to pick up her five-year-old. Already, there was a long line of cars at the Kiss and Ride. She parked on the street and ran to the door where the children exit. It seemed like she was always in a hurry. Today, her son was dragging his feet.

She rushed to get Jason into the car. Anxiety made her heart race, her nerves were on edge, and when he dropped his backpack in the mud, she silently screamed in frustration.

Jason climbed into the car seat, got buckled in, and now her car was blocked by the garbage truck. Fingers drumming the steering wheel, she tried to remember what else she needed to do. Her brain was foggy. What had she forgotten?

The truck finally moved, and she made a dash for home. The chores were waiting—laundry, prepare dinner, clean up, bath time. Being a single working mom meant she had to do it all. There was no help. It had been a hectic day.

Tomorrow would be the same. Parents had been pressuring her to open more gymnastics classes so they could get off the waiting list. She felt helpless and bombarded by questions. What they wanted wasn't possible. In spite of coaching each morning, there was no way she could open up afternoon classes with all the errands she had to do every day.

As she pulled into her driveway, the "check engine" light flashed, reminding her she needed to make a service appointment. There weren't enough hours in the day. When was she going to do that? Can you feel her stress level rising?

Helping her son out of the car seat and up the stairs, she tripped and swore, startling them both. In that moment, she remembered she'd meant to buy soap. Several loads of laundry would have to wait. Sighing, she pushed open the front door, got her son's coat and boots off, settled him with his iPad, and then hurried to the kitchen where she promptly burst into tears.

Anger is a huge emotion. An umbrella label, it can present as anger about something specific, but that code or emotion is usually only the first layer of the onion being peeled away. There will be other variations of it, like a pearl necklace of anger stories. Anger keeps people overwhelmed, running out of time, unable to think clearly because it is like static in their head. People lash out at others in anger.

If there had been another adult in the house, Stacey might have started an argument, saying words she'd later regret.

Benefits of Anger Gone

Stacey had recently met Daniel Flear—the creator of the F.I.X. Code—and had *sad* removed. She was looking forward to seeing him about the code *angry*. With that gone, she knew life would change.

It did.

The day after having *angry* removed, Stacey closed the gym at noon, made a list of her errands, starting with those closest to her gym and working her way to the school for 3:15 p.m. pick up. She ate the lunch she'd made earlier that morning, then headed to the car. You may think this is nothing special, but when you are being controlled by your anger, simple tasks like packing a lunch are impossible.

Stacey's mind was clear, not fuzzy. She knew exactly what she needed to buy in which stores. She stopped by the garage to make an appointment for her car. She was second in line at the Kiss and Ride. She was glad to see her son and heard all of the news of his day. In this one afternoon, she had done all the errands that usually took her five afternoons. She was ecstatic, happy and calm.

The to-do list worked, so she kept it. Because she could now think clearly, she could organize. Since she was organized, her afternoons were free, which meant she could open up new coaching times to eliminate the waiting list. Parents were pleased.

Unexpectedly at the end of the month, there was $600 extra in her bank account. The bank records showed where she had previously spent money frivolously: $110 for Starbucks treats because she was out, $235 for gas as she zig-zagged all over town doing errands, $80 for t-shirts she really didn't need, and $175 for fast food.

What a shock to see how much she casually spent before her extraction of angry. $600 each month adds up over a year. One characteristic of angry is that people indulge in retail therapy, but it is a fleeting relief. Perhaps it's a justification for all the time Stacey devoted to running errands—an unconscious reward.

One characteristic of angry is that people indulge in retail therapy, but it is a fleeting relief.

Without angry, life was smooth and calm. The ease of one afternoon of errands spread to other parts of Stacey's week. With her afternoons freed up, she was able to open up four afternoons for coaching. That cleared up her waiting lists, and the extra income generated was a bonus. Anger was no longer running her life, thanks to the F.I.X. Code. This was a win-win!

If anyone has ever felt overwhelmed and running out of time, they may want to consider that anger is running them. There is only one way I know of to successfully and quickly get life back on track, get rid of the anger, and love your life again. That is with a F.I.X. Code session.

Daniel and Stacey did live trainings for healers, practitioners, mothers, and people like me who wanted to learn this. Most of the class consisted of women looking to add a new technique to their healing practice. They'd had sessions with Stacey and knew this worked. Many of them had children and started to use this technique to help their kids deal with everyday problems of growing up. This changed lives.

The next story is about a mom who desperately needed some way to remove the hurt of several generations.

· CHAPTER 17 ·

Hurt

WHAT HURT LOOKS AND FEELS LIKE

Josefin, an observant and verbal four-year-old, didn't miss anything that went on in the house. She heard everything, saw everything, and remembered it all in the way that children do. Tonight, she was in the family room, having a quiet time. Mom and Dad were in the kitchen talking about money.

Mom and Dad started to talk loudly. Josefin didn't know what money was, but you needed it for toys. Mom said there was no money for a doll she wanted.

"Get a job. You need to make some money to help with all these household bills." Dad waved a handful of papers. "You don't contribute at all."

"And how can I do that? There is no work for me here. And what about Josefin? If we get a sitter for her that would use up all my pay."

"Well, you need to find a way. It's your fault we are always broke. We can't go on like this. It seems like you don't want to work. I can't believe I fell in love with such a loser." His tone of voice was so cross that Josefin jumped. "I hate the sight of you right now." Dad left the house.

Mom ran to the bathroom but not before Josefin saw the tears. She doubled over as if she had been punched in the stomach and started to cry. Mom came back and hugged her until she fell asleep.

Scenes similar to this happen in many homes. Josefin has now watched this one often enough that she knows what hurting people sounds like—she knows the tone of voice and the words like "loser," "hate," and "it's your fault." She knows that when she cries, she gets what she wants. Even if she doesn't have the words, she knows a lot.

That scene is forgotten until the day Mom and Josefin are in the department store. Josefin spies a display of pony toys and immediately chooses the unicorn. She runs to Mom, waving the toy, "I love this one. Please can I have her, Mommy?"

"Sweetie, I am sorry. There is no money for toys today."

Josefin takes one long hard look at Mom, places her hands on her hips, thrusts out her chin, and yells, "I hate you, loser."

Mom's heart shatters. Momentarily flooded with emotions, she is unable to act, stunned into silence. Where had that come from?

Shoppers turn and stare. Hurt is a horrible embarrassment that attacks your confidence. Face flushed, lip trembling, Mom is speechless. She scoops up her daughter and rushes from the store, feeling like her world has ended. She knows how people judge scenes like this; she's done it herself.

Josefin is sobbing. Mom tries to console her, "Oh sweetie. We'll get one next time. You have so many toys at home already. S-h-h-h-h-h. Calm down. Don't cry."

Josefin escalates the crying to tantrum level and covers her ears. Time stands still. People walk slowly by, staring. Finally, Mom makes a decision.

"Okay, honey. It's going to be all right. We'll go back and get the unicorn." The sobbing gets quieter. Inside, ignoring their shopping cart, they carry the unicorn to the checkout. By the time they are home, Mom is exhausted from this emotional rollercoaster. Her mind is racing, trying to figure out what happened as she prepares supper.

Josefin is playing in the living room, clutching the unicorn, smiling and happy.

This is a glimpse of how Josefin may unconsciously navigate life when she is older. Between seven and fourteen, she could be trying out the anger and hurt that she saw around her. One day she may be angry, another day sad, and yet another, hurt. She's trying to find the emotion that works best for her and by fourteen she will have a default behavior that is an unconscious habit.

Children are constantly learning how to communicate their needs. It is a parent's job to help them learn what is appropriate. Kids can manipulate parents because they've learned which behaviors will get them what they want. When this becomes a habit and is the child's default way of communicating their needs in life, it's a problem.

Among other reasons, parents give in out of guilt or trying to keep the peace at all costs or because they take the behavior personally. You or I might have thought the child was manipulating the parent, but with the F.I.X. Code, it is how the parent feels about the problem, not how it looks to anyone else.

We have all seen this because up until age seven, we had no filters. We witnessed scenes with parents and unconsciously stored them away.

A trigger is an event, word, look, or anything else that brings up the feeling. People may be triggers. Often it is words, a look, a tone of voice, a gesture or smell that brings up the feeling. As difficult as it may be to believe, those same things would not likely trigger anyone else.

Finding the code for Mom's feeling is not about what we think we see but about how Mom feels. We cannot assume we know, but there are clues. See what Mom does when she gets home from the store.

We saw how Josefin interpreted the hurt she witnessed at home. In exchange for not being given what she wanted, she hurt back. She used the words, the tone, the look that she had seen Dad use so effectively to make her mother feel hurt only days before.

A mom trained in the F.I.X. Code knows how to handle this situation quickly and easily at bedtime, the first time Dad ever spoke those words. If there were further signs of her being hurt, Josefin's mom would be able to do a session with her.

But Mom didn't know how to do the F.I.X. Code and when Dad walked into the house that evening, he got an earful. It was all his fault. He was horrible to use language like that in front of the child. Mom blamed everything on Dad—not just the event at the store. An angry argument followed, and harsh words that should never have been spoken filled the air.

The child heard it all and likely will carry it forward into her adult life. In the moment, her behavior had gotten her what she wanted. The parents have demonstrated repeatedly that this is what a relationship looks like whether between adults or between children and parents. Josefin will probably be in relationships that resemble her parents. It is also possible that her parents are, to some extent, living out the relationship of their own parents.

Hurt Becomes Anger

Hurt often appears like a bullet hitting a person's heart.

Hurt often appears like a bullet hitting a person's heart. It takes their breath away, and they feel the hit. A few minutes later, as they think about the hurt, they begin to blame the other person for doing this to them. People become hurtful and vengeful. They may even plot out their revenge.

The thought is to hurt back, to retaliate. This does not go away easily. Josefin's mom was hurt, and as this changed to anger, she blamed Dad. She said so.

It is possible to see the hurt cycle begin in teenage relationships and continue into adult years. For example, at seventeen, Sue is hurt when her boyfriend Jackson is seen talking to another girl. To make the hurt stop, after telling him off, she breaks up with Jackson. However, her hurt doesn't go away. Sue thinks the only way not to feel hurt any longer is to go back to Jackson. They reunite.

When a photo is posted to social media, Sue is hurt again. He is out with friends one evening without her. The cycle continues. It escalates when Sue retaliates by spreading gossip about one of the friends in the photo.

Or perhaps, Sue finds another partner similar to Jackson, only to repeat the cycle until she learns how to break it by going through a series of therapy sessions, or she has a fifteen-minute F.I.X. Code session.

One side effect of being hurt by someone is that the hurt person knows how to hurt other people. It may be an unconscious knowing, but it is real.

Remember Josefin saying, "I hate you!" to her mom? She knows how to hurt because she has seen and heard her parents hurt each other. Perhaps she has been unintentionally hurt by someone else she loves. Seeing Mom's reaction to Dad's loser comments, she knows now how to push Mom's buttons and trigger that reaction. We saw the external signs of Mom's embarrassment, like the flushed face and the desire to flee from the scene. Embarrassment stifles confidence. Mom was afraid of ridicule and what others might think of her.

Several different feelings surged through Mom in a short while—ask any parent if they have felt that way. Or think of a time when you were faced with such opposition from a child that you felt helpless. I remember such an event clearly.

In an emergency, I picked up a friend's five-year-old from school. Tanya was visibly angry that Mom wasn't there and proceeded to push every button I had forgotten I had. She shouted songs about the toilet at the top of her lungs as we drove. She kicked the back of my seat and threw her boots at me.

I had years of experience with young children but never anything like this. I am still in awe at her power to disable me. As a principal, I had been able to silence an auditorium of students within seconds, but not this kindergarten student. She was taking out her anger at her mom on me. I was not going to win.

I couldn't decide what to do. For a moment, I felt torn in different directions yet paralyzed, helpless. Maybe that is to avoid making a rash decision. Eventually I pulled the car to the curb, saying, "I know you're upset that Mom is sick, but it's not safe to drive when you act like this. When you are singing quietly, we'll go home to see Mom."

I did consider for hours afterward how I could have handled this differently. Maybe I needed a refresher course in kid's behavior, but mostly I hoped I never had to pick her up again.

If she were my child, I'd deal with her behavior as soon as it first appeared. But I had watched her own mother feel helpless and unable to act. This girl knew how to express her hurt and anger, which gave her power over me. It was a humbling experience to be at the mercy of a five-year-old.

Hurt has the same energy as anger. Josefin's mom immediately felt the hurt in her heart. We know Mom was hurt because she blamed Dad for what happened as soon as he walked through the door. With hurt, eventually Mom came to the conclusion that because Josefin heard Dad say those words, it was his fault this happened.

If Mom had only been embarrassed, perhaps she might have left the store with the child and driven home to avoid the stares and judgment of others. But Mom also felt the guilt of not being able to give her daughter what she wanted and went back into the store to purchase the toy. Because she felt guilty, she gave in.

It isn't always clear which emotion it is in the moment, and as an observer, we can only guess. Most of this happens on the unconscious level so that we feel the intensity of emotion, not just one single feeling.

Benefits of Hurt Gone

Without this feeling of hurt, it is possible to feel compassion for others because people may understand that the one hurting them has been hurt in the past. It also means that the feelings of hurt, anger, and blaming the other person are not necessary.

People don't have to hurt back and in fact, the comment that used to hurt them, may be ignored. They may not feel insulted. That is hard to believe. In fact, it doesn't make any sense without this experience. When I was told I wouldn't care if my husband interrupted my work in the darkroom now that my feeling of guilt was gone, I didn't believe that could happen. However, it was true. I had to accept that I had changed.

As a parent not feeling hurt, it is possible to do what is best for the child. Parents will not be embarrassed into submission, into buying unnecessary toys when money is tight. Mom will be able to have a conversation with her four-year-old to show she understands the child is upset and then handle the situation differently.

Perhaps Mom will make a plan to buy the unicorn another time and teach Josefin about saving for it. Maybe Grandma sends one as a gift. There are many ways to avoid setting Josefin up to expect instant gratification. Retail therapy isn't necessary if these codes are eliminated.

If a parent cannot or does not discipline their child, what is the prognosis for that child in life? The seeds of the codes are planted in childhood by parents, family, at day care and school, from shows on television and videos, or by anyone the child has contact with. These fears, anxieties, and other emotions can be passed from generation to generation simply because if they were not dealt with, they become part of life and may be acted out for a lifetime.

If the nightly newscast is any indicator, it seems that society is not well equipped to deal with these negative emotions. What is in place within schools and classrooms can be improved. One of the youngest practitioners certified at the first live F.I.X. Code training was a fourteen-year-old. She routinely used this technique on her friends. If they were having a bad day for any reason, she wouldn't let them wallow in it. They would find a quiet corner and do the F.I.X. Code protocol. That would be the end of that negativity.

· CHAPTER 18 ·

Guilt

WHAT GUILT LOOKS AND FEELS LIKE

Since I already told you my guilt story about being interrupted in the darkroom, let's see how guilt can look in other situations. I also want to describe briefly the Grand Illusion because likely you've experienced it.

The Grand Illusion keeps us believing that if we could have acted differently, events would have had better results. We don't believe that we were doing our best with what resources and knowledge we had. Intellectually we know, but our unconscious mind tells us differently.

How could we have done better? I fell victim to this when a favorite aunt died. She had relied on family for years to keep her independent and to look after her in illness. Despite being with her in the hospital every moment I could and doing everything possible, I felt that it hadn't been enough. I beat myself up while knowing that it was futile to think I could have changed the outcome. To me, this is the Grand Illusion triggered by guilt.

My first session with Stacey was all about my code *"guilt."* It surprised me when it came up. I had cut short my work time in the darkroom because I felt guilty about not spending time with my husband. He didn't consciously know that. I was aware that he was missing his friend, and I was not there to support him. There were other examples of guilt when I thought about it. Yes, I had a necklace made of guilty stories. My guilt button was right there, ready to be pushed.

For each of the big umbrella emotions, there are many single emotions. Anger, hurt, and embarrassment sit under the umbrella of *anger*. They have a similar vibration, but they are different feelings. *Guilt* is a sister code to *sad*.

Guilt keeps us in the past as we replay the same event over and over, falsely believing we could have changed the outcome, imagining a different scenario, wishing we had acted differently, had not said something, feeling like we don't deserve to be happy or receive a gift. It keeps us static.

I should have spent more time with my aunt, I should have called more often, I should have done more for her, I should have spoken with her doctor sooner, I should have asked for a second medical opinion—all part of the Grand Illusion.

Guilt is like a huge red button labelled "Push me." It is so easy to have it pushed by a word, a tone of voice, a phrase, or a look. You can feel great one moment and be guilt ridden the next. Children are masters at pushing the guilt button, if you have one. We see kids push the parent's guilt button all the time. Just observe when you are in a store.

With the F.I.X. Code, you can get rid of that guilt button or any other button that sets you off. You deal with the negative emotion associated with the problem in the moment. Sometimes they overlap, like guilt and sad might.

Benefits of Guilt Gone

With my own guilt gone, I understood that I didn't need to give up my darkroom time, that I could find a way to solve the problem. Before that, it looked impossible, and I felt I was the one to have to change. While I did change, I didn't feel like this had been imposed upon me.

Without guilt, people can parent differently. It's possible to talk rationally; they don't feel like a bad person. They can be a positive role model. Parents are not guilted into agreeing to things they later regret or feeling pressured to give in to the demands of their children or buying expensive items to appease them.

People get away with all kinds of behavior because they push others' guilt buttons. Let's face it, people are thinking about themselves and what they want. They aren't thinking about how their actions affect others. No one else knows why we act as we do, or why we do things for others, especially if guilt is a trigger.

The trigger can be unknown. One person sets off the trigger, and the other guilt-ridden one reacts. Once guilt is up and running, the situation can deteriorate quickly. The guilty person may feel railroaded and then angry—at themselves or at the one who pushed their button.

Guilt keeps people regretting events and their actions. They mistakenly think they could have done better, done more, helped more or been a better friend.

With guilt, they feel helpless because they cannot fix the past. Guilt keeps them awake at night, self-sabotaging or overcompensating, feeling that they caused the problem or did something wrong. No one else has to know they feel guilty in order for them to act out of guilt. This one had been a long-standing theme for me.

With guilty, people do things they don't want to do—such as staying in a relationship. Guilt allows people to be indebted to others and therefore guilted into anything. For example, if their partner makes them feel guilty because of working long hours and not being home with the children, then they may be guilted into doing something to compensate like organizing an expensive vacation or purchasing unnecessary items. The absentee guilt-ridden parent may be run ragged by the kids when home.

If a wife cheats on her partner, he may feel guilty for losing money at the casino and start to believe this is the reason she cheated on him. Now that he feels guilty, she has power over him even if the wife is not consciously aware.

This is a powerful code. Guilt keeps a person feeling indebted to someone else, feeling owned, even if the other person is not aware. With the fear of feeling guilty, spontaneity disappears. People weigh all the ramifications before acting and consider their words carefully before speaking. But with guilt gone, it is possible to say what needs to be said and not worry that each word will hurt others.

> *Guilt keeps a person feeling indebted to someone else, feeling owned, even if the other person is not aware.*

Guilt is tied to self-sabotage. When people are guilt-ridden, they are unaware that guilt drives their actions. With guilt gone, there is no need to deprive or punish themselves. "No" is an acceptable response. Excuses are not necessary. They can accept that they have done their best, and they are responsible for themselves.

Without guilt, people can be in control and confident. Their feelings about themselves change, and they can experience the goodness life offers. Eliminating guilt is freeing and powerful.

· CHAPTER 19 ·

Sad

WHAT SAD LOOKS AND FEELS LIKE

Sad and guilt are sister codes. They interconnect much of the same content but feel different. Sad involves disappointment, loss, and grief. Josefin's mom may have felt sad about the state of her marriage, her lack of employment, or other common concerns.

Emily is a busy mom with a full-time career. Her birthday, July 3, has been overshadowed by her Mom's birthday on June 30. Emily is pre-occupied on her birthday, thinking of her mother who died several years ago. She is so sad she doesn't want to be with anyone, yet the family insists.

Emily confided, "I hate my birthday. I want to be alone, and the family bugs me to go shopping for gifts I don't really want. This year I was so angry at myself for being such a rude mom that I said okay to whatever they showed me and ended up with enough new makeup to last a lifetime. Last year it was underwear and the year before, chocolates."

Because Emily gives in to the family, she is angry at herself and acts like someone she doesn't know. She doesn't enjoy her birthday.

"I feel guilty for not wanting to celebrate with everyone. I really just want to be left alone to cry. Do you know how difficult it is to pretend to smile when you want to cry instead? It takes a lot of effort. I am already in a bad mood. I can't enjoy our time together. Whatever they want to do is fine. I don't care."

Emily actually labeled the codes herself and between her words, behavior, and body language, I knew she was experiencing *sad*. She admitted she felt guilty, is still grieving her mother, and disappointment in her own behavior is part of this.

The reason why she would be sad is obvious but with the F.I.X. Code, it doesn't matter. I don't have to ask her for the details. She doesn't have to relive events and describe them to me. The content of the backstory is irrelevant. Her body language has always indicated a sadness, but she has never discussed this with me before.

Sad is almost impossible to shake. It's isolating. Everything about a sad person is droopy and sad looking. The muscles in the face are elongated, the eyes droop, the cheeks are hollow, the shoulders slump. If a friend is telling her sad story, she looks sad. You know the look.

In order to change the feeling, sad people often eat alone or brings treats to work. The weight piles on as they eat to feel happy, trying to change their environment. If eating doesn't change their state of being, they want to go to bed and pull the covers over their head.

Sad steals joy, laughter, and fun. It is a low vibration—sluggish, weak, and tired, people's knees buckle under the weight of the sadness. It's safe at home, so people isolate themselves. Any sense of humor disappears. It is an exhausting, heavy feeling. Everything feels like an effort. The world doesn't feel safe or comfortable.

Benefits of Sad Gone

We did the F.I.X. Code session to remove Emily's *sad*. The immediate result was that sad was gone. Emily will smile, her body language and posture will change. She won't look as though she is carrying the weight of the world on her shoulders.

The real proof will come on her next birthday although by then I predict she will have forgotten about the *sad* code she had removed and will enjoy her day out with her family, not wishing to be home alone with her head under the blanket.

After a F.I.X. Code experience, people still feel appropriate emotions. If someone is sad, they will feel it, but it is not a lifetime of sadness. Emily will still feel the sadness of losing her mom. However, she won't dwell on this on her birthday, and she will share the family's fun of celebrating. All her sad stories will not come up to spoil her day. The string of her *sad* necklace has been broken.

When *sad* and *hurt* are combined, a person moves toward isolation and depression. Many people who find the F.I.X. Code are depressed. Some of the first big codes removed are sad and hurt, and clients are not depressed after that. When sad is removed, it is possible to want to be out in public again.

When *sad* is gone, people may find their cheeks hurt because their smile is genuine and constant. They no longer need to be alone, isolated, hiding out, and sad. The vicious cycle stops when *sad* is gone.

All the muscles go back in place and are used as they are meant to be used. The years fall away. People look years younger. It is the best face lift ever!

Lonely is about feeling alone even when surrounded by people. There is so much disconnect and isolation in our lives. These days, a glass of wine seems to make us feel less alone as does our mobile phone. Telling sad stories with friends over wine, thinking you are being there for each other is not support. Momentarily, it may seem so, but all that talking about the problem anchors the feelings in.

With *sad* gone by using the F.I.X. Code, conversation changes to things that are more pleasant. Life is no longer about consoling each other, but about enjoying friends.

When someone changes after a F.I.X. Code session, their stories are now irrelevant. They may no longer have the patience for others' sad stories or sad people any longer. Relationships change. This can be a process that requires some adjustment, or it can happen quickly, but people are able to make the changes they need to.

Our final code is an important one that many people wouldn't identify at first. Like the others, it can be subtle and have many symptoms.

· CHAPTER 20 ·

Betrayal and Rejection

Relationships are built on trust and our lives are all about relationships.

Betrayal is a powerful yet subtle code. If you hear people second guessing themselves, that is a clue that *betrayal* is a code for them. It can be dealt with when it comes up in a F.I.X. Code session. Their words may be "not trusting" or "second guessing." Both are symptoms of betrayal.

As you read, remember that these codes are triggered by personal events or incidents. People may not want to admit they have been betrayed because it changes lives. They may not realize that betrayal triggers others around them. People may be unaware that their actions or words might cause emotions to surface in others. Remember too that what elicits the feeling of betrayal in one person won't trigger it for another.

Raising Well-Adjusted Children

Most parents aspire to raise well adjusted, responsible children who grow to be productive members of society. Research supports parenting with unconditional love and firm discipline. If a parent is being run by the emotions of betrayal or rejection, this affects all their relationships, especially as they are role models for their children. This applies to any lesson that ultimately prepares children for life. It could be as simple as saying "thank you," telling the truth, respecting parents, or doing homework.

Parenting is not an easy job and for most people, knowing how to parent is a skill they acquired from their own parents. So much information is researched, written, and available about parenting styles. There are also some types of parenting styles that appear to be beneficial but actually may not be helpful.

I am thinking of several styles I have witnessed, such as "helicopter," "drone," or "snow plow" parenting. The most recent term, snow plow, describes how a parent removes any obstacle in their child's way. Parents do this for their own reasons, often believing they are helpful when really what they are doing is teaching their children that they are not capable of learning to problem solve. That may not be the parents' intention, but if they harbor unconscious feelings of betrayal, they are prone to raising children who feel powerless or not trusted. Eventually the children give in and act as the parent expects them to—helpless, purposely forgetful or ignoring a request. It is possible for the child to unconsciously seek power by taking their behavior to the extreme, perhaps becoming an omnipotent child. This is not what most parents want.

THE F.I.X. CODE

> *It is possible for the child to unconsciously seek power by taking their behavior to the extreme, perhaps becoming an omnipotent child.*

Rather than removing all obstacles from a child's life or solving all problems for the child, teaching them how to deal with the problems will serve them better as they mature. But to do this, a parent can't be run by betrayal that has them second guessing or not trusting all the time.

As a teacher, I faced these parents often. At lunch time, Mom grilled her six-year-old about every negative moment at school then complained to me that another child had said something mean to her daughter. It was taken out of context. My advice was for Mom to stop asking leading questions such as, "What did that horrible Clayton do to you this morning?" and ask, "What was the best thing about this morning?"

As a principal, I dealt with one parent who complained in person at 8:45 a.m. about an incident the day before involving her fourteen-year old who had sworn at the teacher. The parent stated it was the fault of the teacher. Twenty minutes later, mother called me to ask how the issue had been resolved, sure that her child was a victim. At that time of day, students were entering the school, getting books from lockers, and all teachers were busy getting the classes settled. During that twenty minutes, I had been involved with the morning office routines. The snow plow parent was now angry at me because the issue was not resolved.

Here are a few of the thoughts I had about this. First, the student knew Mom would fight her battles no matter how she behaved. Second, Mom didn't trust her child to be able to speak for herself and take responsibility for her actions. Third, Mom didn't trust me to absolve her child of blame for swearing at the teacher. Perhaps she had a suspicion that there was no excusable reason.

Mom, while being run by several codes, was also looking to place blame, thus setting her daughter up for many complex feelings that will show up later in life.

What Betrayal Looks and Feels Like

Imagine the ramifications if the betrayal involves something more significant than a spouse running an errand or kids doing their homework. I am not suggesting that every parent or person is affected by the code *betrayal*. I am trying to provide some scenarios that help readers understand how complicated life can be when any of these codes run a person, whether it is the parent, a spouse, a friend, or a child.

You met Jan and Bill in Chapter 1. Jan kept in touch with me as she grew up. She dropped out of school when she was sixteen and became a waitress then a hairdresser before meeting her husband. She was fortunate to have had caring grandparents who supported her emotionally during this time.

Now with two young children, Jan finds parenting to be a challenge and doesn't want to make the mistakes her parents made. However, she always felt that her father had left her to start another family—a huge betrayal in her eyes. Much as she said she loves her half-brothers and her step-mom, her actions show that she is being unconsciously run by the code *betrayal*.

Betrayal can be about anything—breaking a promise, telling a secret, a partner stealing funds from the business, or an extramarital affair. Let's look at how a person who has been betrayed at some point in life, may react to events that could be coincidental.

Jan became suspicious about Bill's absences from home at odd times. Why is he so forgetful about the errands? She wonders why he is constantly checking his messages. Who is he texting while they watch TV? Why does he always take his phone with him? She starts to ask friends about him. Have they had coffee recently? She asks Bill about the friends, still looking for discrepancies in his story. This sounds over the top if you aren't run by betrayal, but it is not that extreme if you are.

Shortly after this, mutual friend Vanessa casually mentioned to Jan that she saw Bill at the movies. He never saw Vanessa as he was in line at the snack bar. Later Jan mentioned the encounter to Bill who looked puzzled. Because Jan is being run by the *betrayal* code, she is certain he is covering up an affair. Her mind goes into overdrive. She imagines a whole scenario then looks for supporting evidence.

She stalks Vanessa on social media, looking for clues that Bill is seeing her. Jan asks crazy questions when Bill is late after work. She asks her kids if Dad has met friends when they are all at the movies with him. It becomes impossible to trust him.

Her actions spill over into the relationship. Bill is now feeling victimized. Neither of them trusts each other. The suspicions create confusion and mistrust in Jan's head. She makes it worse by constantly searching for incongruencies in his story.

It's why people hire private detectives. Suspicion at the discrepancies—whether real, circumstantial, or imagined—can drive one's life. Once suspicious about betrayal, can that be forgiven? Can people forgive and forget, move on together?

It is possible with the F.I.X. Code.

Let's take this scenario further. Without betrayal running you, this may sound far-fetched, but how do you judge another person's thoughts and feelings if you don't have the same emotional code running you?

If a relationship doesn't work out after a betrayal, separation may be next. People say that time heals the wounds and in time they will forget. This belief is seldom accurate. The wounds may fade, but people carry that unconscious belief that they are about to be betrayed into future relationships.

The damage spreads to other parts of their life. As role models, parents teach adult behavior to their children. As the children grow up and date, they unconsciously model their relationship on what they saw around them. This is especially evident when as adults they vow, usually unsuccessfully, to be different from their parents.

Do we unconsciously search for a partner that gives us the same kind of relationship that we, as children, witnessed with our own parents? Is this why it is said that people marry their parent? Is it possible for adults to end relationships over small incidents and unintentionally model for the children that relationships don't involve respect, hard work, or challenges? Is it possible to stay too long in loveless or abusive relationships and model to our children that this is what a relationship looks like? I believe it is.

Is it possible for adults to end relationships over small incidents and unintentionally model for the children that relationships don't involve respect, hard work, or challenges?

As an educator, I often counseled children whose parents were in the process of separating. Six-year-olds did not understand the situation. Fourteen-year-olds could be bitter yet still hoped their parents would reunite. As a F.I.X. Code practitioner, it was common to hear 45-year-olds say they still wished for the family to be one unit. A divorce was often the source of this person's feeling of betrayal.

This subject deserves more attention.

Micromanaging

In a simple form of betrayal, people are constantly micromanaging. One person is almost nagging, hovering or acting like a drone—constantly surveillant. This prevents the other from being a true partner in the relationship.

With the kids, constantly nagging teaches them to fail. It may be over something as simple as putting their boots in the closet, not leaving them all over the hall floor. Every time the boots are a mess and someone else tidies the mess, the message to the children is that they are not capable of doing this themselves the "right way." Eventually the kids will prove that they are not capable and exhibit the behavior that is expected of them. They stop picking up the boots. It is the job of someone else—probably Mother.

Betrayal Is a Double-Edged Sword

Betrayal is a double-edged sword. One edge is about trust. For anyone who has been betrayed or believes they have been betrayed, it's not possible to trust the words or actions of others. It's difficult to believe the truth. This can be crazy making because a person is always on guard, constantly looking for incongruencies or lies in words and actions. It's hard work to save a relationship that involves betrayal.

When the F.I.X. Code extraction is done and betrayal is gone, trust is possible. People no longer feel betrayed. It's not necessary to work through this. When the code of betrayal is gone, clear thinking means it's easier to make decisions without second guessing choices. It could be as simple as being confident that the parking spot at the mall is satisfactory and that the car does not have to be moved several times.

The second edge of the betrayal sword is that trusting in self is not possible. When people are overly vigilant or never confident of their decisions, they change their minds often. They second guess and find it difficult to commit to a plan or choice. They try to gain control by gathering all the details, just as Jan did about Bill's activities. They scrutinize, looking for places where the story doesn't make sense, believing this proves they are being lied to. Once a person has been betrayed, it's not easy to repair this.

Forgiveness is difficult. Betrayal steals joy from life as people expect the worst. The code, betrayal, changes how information is processed and how life is perceived. Everything is seen through a filter of betrayal. People change.

After confrontation about a betrayal, it's common to feel foolish, embarrassed, and naïve. People can act out of character, saying and doing things that they usually would not and embarrassed when they recall their response. For example, when Bill walked in without the milk that first night, he was embarrassed. He tried to make excuses, and his words started an argument that lasted for days and set the tone for future conversations.

Once betrayed, trusting self is difficult. People ignore their instincts and second guess their decisions. Remember betrayal is a double-edged sword. First you don't trust others, but then you second guess your own decisions. It may be understandable to not trust others. Not trusting yourself may sound far-fetched, but both are linked. No one wants to be fooled into making the wrong decision again. How does one decide who or what to trust after that?

Betrayal is a double-edged sword. First you don't trust others, but then you second guess your own decisions

---

Have you ever met a person who was unable to make a decision or appeared to be timid about life in general? This issue can undermine a person's life and show up in the most unusual ways depending on what triggers the code. This can limit life. They are constantly re-evaluating choices, over and over: "I can't make up my mind which birthday card to buy. They are all perfect. I like this musical one, but the verse on this one is nicer. I'll get the musical one. Oh, here's one that is funny. I'll get it instead."

I believe that taken to its extreme, this betrayal and lack of trust can look like paranoia. After a manufacturer recalls a product, I have heard people say they won't purchase that item or brand in the future. They've lost trust in that supplier and refuse to buy the product again. They will do without rather than take a chance that the items are unsafe.

One final word about Jan. She was fortunate to have had a strong support system. She went back to school and as part of her own healing process, became a personal support worker. She is in service to those who need care and personal attention. This training and experience have allowed her to revisit many of her own values and motives while navigating life. She is nearing the age where people often come up against obstacles unlike any they have met before. Only time will tell how Jan handles the next part of life.

REJECTION

Betrayal can also lead to *rejection*. When rejected, that person may go away emotionally wounded and never recover. They may become passive aggressive and cyberbully or stalk the offender, or they can fight back with all their might—or any behavior in between.

Rejection can become a violent code. There is often a visceral reaction when a person is rejected. If a partner walks away from the relationship saying it's over, the rejected person can feel as though they've been kicked in the stomach. A response to that can seem out of proportion, resulting in reports of road rage, gun violence, and physical attacks.

BENEFITS OF BETRAYAL GONE

When the feelings attached to this emotion are gone, trust is possible. How it happens depends on the client. They may shed the anger attached to that betrayal. While they may not immediately trust their betrayer, they may feel some compassion for them, knowing the other had felt betrayed at some time.

The reaction to betrayal can range from obvious to subtle and puzzling. I have seen victims act like survivors of abuse, constantly trying to please the betrayer. Others have left the relationship. Or there may be a vague feeling of not knowing how to act around the betrayer. With that gone, the memory of the event is still there, but it becomes manageable. The victim of betrayal may be able to see what role they played in the events.

> *The reaction to betrayal can range from obvious to subtle and puzzling. I have seen victims act like survivors of abuse, constantly trying to please the betrayer. Others have left the relationship.*

As unlikely as this may seem, it is possible for people to trust again, starting with themselves. Imagine making a decision and not giving it a second thought!

Once betrayal is gone—thinking is clear, action oriented, and does not focus on micromanaging. Parents no longer have to hover or nag. They set an example so that the children have appropriate role models. They demonstrate trust to the family so children can grow to have trusting relationships in the future.

There is no need to obsess about others, constantly texting reminders, checking up, stalking on social media, or looking for lies and incongruencies in stories. Relationships become partnerships. It is possible to move forward in life no longer paralyzed with indecision.

The family can have healthy relationships, feel that they are good enough, and that forgetting the quart of milk is not a big deal. What a relief that would be! Just think about all the arguments and hassles in life that could be avoided. People would not notice all those little annoyances that previously demanded so much attention.

A Musical Trigger for Betrayal

Gail called me to talk about an article she was writing. It marks a turning point in her career because she's hesitant to share so much personal information. Years ago, her sister had read her diary entries. That had been such an invasion of privacy. The feeling of betrayal has stayed with Gail and was the reason she chose a career other than writing. Now, she was willing to write a 200-word essay as a first step toward a dream.

"My writing coach said I need to stop apologizing for my feelings. They are mine. I don't see how I'm apologizing. I never wrote the word sorry."

The coach had explained that once Gail had stated her feeling in the story, she then discounted it by implying that other character's feelings were more important.

"That isn't my intention, but I don't want to change that. The other person's feelings are important to the story."

Three days passed. Gail had not touched the manuscript. "I'll put it away for a few more days and think about it."

We spoke later that week. She had not written another word since the conversation with the coach but had awakened that morning with music and words to a song running through her head, "Private Eyes are Watching You" by Hall and Oates.

She concluded, "I guess I am not ready to put my personal life out there."

That made sense. "How do you feel about writing the article?

"My words have no value."

There was the code for her session.

What could be worse for a writer than believing there is no value in her writing? This belief takes away all her purpose, the pleasure of creating, the satisfaction of a well-crafted sentence, and any desire to honor the writer within.

With that code gone, Gail completed her edits and kept on writing!

· CHAPTER 21 ·

I'm a Student Again

Ding, ding! A text announced the first live training course for the F.I.X. Code Technique. Wanting to support Stacey in bringing this technique to a wider audience, I texted back, "Count me in!"

I didn't plan on being a practitioner. Even so, I was a bit anxious when we were asked to partner up to give each other a F.I.X. Code session. We had observed Daniel working with several participants that weekend. He gave us the protocol for doing this work, but I still had my doubts. Would it work for me?

We gained rapport with our partners and began the process. I read the instructions out loud. When it was over, it had worked. My partner's feeling of sadness was gone. From the comments I overheard, it seemed others were also surprised at their success. Apparently learning to do the F.I.X. Code as a practitioner was just as easy as reaping the benefits of it.

Over the next three months, I did a hundred sessions with strangers while I learned the script and became comfortable with the process. The most common emotions that people were anxious to eliminate were anger and rage, sadness, anxiety, and betrayal. There were also many feelings related to personal inadequacies that might have been symptoms of those common emotions. Each time, at the end of the session, when I asked if the client could feel that negative emotion that had been their code, the answer was "No." I was pleased for them.

Working with many people gave me insight into the type of emotions that people carry with them for long periods of time. Most of my clients were women, and the root causes of their codes had some commonalities. Many were around relationships with their own self-image and the image they presented to the world. It affected how they were treated by others and their partners and—because of the symbiotic nature of relationships—how they treated other people both consciously and unconsciously.

Often people expressed a regret and sadness that they had not lived their life to the fullest, that they had settled for less than they wanted, which could mean unfulfilled relationships, unsuitable jobs, careers, the wrong education, or dreams that never came true. Several women spoke of abuse, being weighed down by responsibilities, feeling guilty about not being able to conceive a child, or having a miscarriage. The underlying sadness they carried with them about these life events was evident in their appearance.

After a F.I.X. Code session, the memory of these events remained.

People have their feelings in the moment, but because the sadness, guilt or hurt that had been with them a lifetime was gone,

THE F.I.X. CODE

there is no reason for the memories to come up uninvited. Life had been viewed through a filter of sadness, guilt, or hurt. With the filter removed, those memories can remain tucked away. People do not have to live in the past with their memories anymore. That feeling kept them from moving forward and with it gone, their life changes.

Photos are images of memories. If a filter is placed over a photo, the perception changes. In some cases, certain colors disappear. One filter, *sad*, changes feelings about the picture. It is the same picture, but it isn't the true picture. It becomes a new reality. Remove the filter and the picture changes again. The F.I.X Code removes that sad filter. The picture of the event remains, but the impression of the picture changes. With the filter removed, the picture is clear, real, and the feelings in the moment that photo was taken are available, no longer overlaid with sadness. You adjust your view of the picture. Because the *sad* filter is gone, you won't be thinking of that picture anymore, and if you do see it, you won't feel the same degree of sadness about it.

To be trusted by these strangers with their deepest emotions, even a single code word about their feelings, was an honor. I felt such empathy and compassion. We all have burdens, but I realized that we never know what anyone else is carrying. I had been raised to be strong and silent. It is a flawed template if it means I don't understand that I can ask for help in dealing with my feelings.

The success of the F.I.X. Code Technique was encouraging. A couple of difficult situations taught me that if people don't want to really change, if their involvement was only to help me, or if they weren't honest about how they felt about their biggest problem, then this would not work well.

But for those who want to change, this will work and it changes lives. Imagine not carrying around *sad* or *angry* all the time! Life would be different.

My own codes from childhood were with me as an adult. I had never learned to deal with my negative emotions. Instead, I had learned to hide my feelings, believing they would go away, to live up to the expectations of others, and to never give up.

I had done major work through counseling, reading, and other means to correct, remove, or overcome these habits. It was only when I had my F.I.X. Code sessions that I could see that all past efforts had been in preparation to experience this technique that worked for me.

The science that our emotions affect our stress level, which impacts our physical well-being, has been around since the 1970s. It has been proven repeatedly as it has been refined. This cannot be ignored. Chronic stress has been shown to alter the immune system, making it less effective at protecting your body. Exposure to a variety of stressors such as I experienced in a short time—moving from familiar to unfamiliar schools, loss of family members, a demanding job—can lead to burnout.

Esther Sternberg, writes in *The Balance Within* that "some studies are beginning to show that burnt-out patients may have not only a psychological burnout but also physiological burnout." She continues on to say that chronic unrelenting stress can change the stress response itself and other hormonal changes. The effects are more serious for women, as "recurring and extended episodes of depression result in permanent changes in bone structure— weakening of bones and osteoporosis of the same degree as a menopausal woman twice her age." (Sternberg 2001)

Dr. Sternberg is respected globally as an authority on the mind-body connection. She states that stress makes people sick by preventing the immune system from doing its job of allowing them to heal, and she explains how.

Memories with attached emotions can cause stress. If this stress becomes chronic, it seems we are setting ourselves up for disease. My doctor was on the right track when she told me to quit my job, although it was too late to avoid the physical damage of arthritis caused by stress. I had bilateral knee replacement surgery shortly after burning out.

I appreciate that there is science to back up the stress-emotion-illness connection. Knowing intuitively from my own experience that this link exists is one thing, but having the scientific proof is important in supporting the evolution of our beliefs.

Having the F.I.X. Code change how I feel about the emotions attached to old memories is healing me. I am able to experience the joy of living in the "now." There is immense satisfaction in being involved in my own recovery and being able to discard that emotional baggage. I have sent that lion under the bed away—forever. My life will continue to evolve as I do.

I believe that my changes will influence the world.

Not only has my life changed, but so have the lives of people I have touched. If each of them in turn adapts and initiates change in themselves, imagine how far can this effect can travel.

> *"Those who are crazy enough to think they can change the world usually do."*
> —Steve Jobs

References

Esther M. Sternberg, M.D. *The Balance Within: The Science Connecting Health and Emotions.* New York: W.H. Freeman and Company, 2001

Eckhart Tolle. *The Power of Now.* Vancouver, BC: Namaste Publishing Inc., 1997.

Joshua@experiencegenie.org "Eckhart Tolle's Top Tips for a Magic Life." 6 February 2017. <http://www.iamgenie.org/eckhart-tolles-top-tips-for-a-magic-life/>

https://www.webmd.com/balance/stress-management/features/10-fixable-stress-related-health-problems#1

https://staceynye.com

https://danielflear.com

https://thefixcode.com

> *"In a gentle way, you can shake the world."*
> —Mahatma Gandhi

For me, that gentle way is the F.I.X. Code. Can it help you too?

About Cory Stickley

Cory Stickley is a student of life, constantly moving toward the next thing that enriches her life. It is easy to see how her career and interests have led her to writing this book, to delving into the "why" behind things that happen, although she has often said she never knowingly aspired to write.

Experiencing the F.I.X. Code technique changed her life. Facilitating change for others, enabling them to be happy, free of anger or anxieties, is empowering for a practitioner. Knowing there is relief for your own pain or blockage relieves stress and sets you free of fears. Cory admits that she had several F.I.X. Code sessions to overcome these feelings while writing.

Fascinated by behavior, the unconscious mind, and personality, Cory has written about her personal experiences and how these elements can come together in life—often leading to frustration or feelings of inadequacy. Life is about relationship. This technique is a way to improve those interactions, much as Cory changed hers—seemingly with no effort. You can do that, too.

> "Look for the good—it is everywhere."
> —Daniel Flear

You are welcome to contact Cory at this email address: LivingAFixedLife@gmail.com.

Made in the USA
Coppell, TX
06 November 2025

62694100R00085